AT THE EDGE
— OF A —
HEARTBEAT

Based on a True Story

Brian Pellegrino

NEWMAN SPRINGS PUBLISHING
320 Broad Street
Red Bank, NJ 07701

First originally published by Newman
Springs Publishing 2022

ISBN 978-1-63881-939-4 (Paperback)
ISBN 978-1-63881-940-0 (Digital)

Printed in the United States of America

CHAPTER 1

WE ALL GO TO BED at night never truly knowing what the next morning might bring. Sure, we have a general idea: get ready for work, get the kids ready for school, and maybe go to the gym. Everyone has their daily routine, but with each new day comes with it an untold number of unforeseen circumstances. You may finally get that promotion you'd been hoping for. Today might be the day you meet your soul mate. You might even win the lottery, or…one day, you may wake up to one of the worst experiences of your life. One fateful morning, I woke up to a scene that would forever be burned into the back of my mind.

It was early December. My dad and I went in search of the perfect Christmas tree. He always insisted on getting a real tree. He didn't believe in that "artificial crap," as he called it. The only time we could go was on a Sunday afternoon. My dad had been working seven days a week without any days off since Halloween so he and my mom could afford to buy Christmas gifts for my brother and me. He worked very hard to provide the best for us. He cut his shift short that day so that he would be home by the early afternoon. My dad worked at the Triboro Bus Company in Queens for the last thirty-seven years, first as a driver and now as a dispatcher. It was about a twenty-mile drive from our house on Long Island. His shift started at 4:00 a.m., so he had to wake up no later than three o'clock to get there in time. The good thing about leaving so early is that he never had to deal with the horrendous morning rush-hour traffic. All those years going in so early and traveling so far were starting to take a toll. At nearly sixty years old, he was close to retirement. He could have retired earlier, but he wanted to get as many years under his belt as he could to boost the amount in his monthly pension checks.

He looked good for sixty. He still had all of his hair with no grays in sight, not even in his mustache, which, oddly enough, was brown, compared to the hair on his head, which was jet-black. My dad always seemed to have a tan. We were Italian, so he had naturally dark skin, plus he loved to sit in the sun during the summer.

With the sun setting, we found our tree and put it on the roof of my car. My dad wasn't going to put it on the roof of his Cadillac, but my twenty-year-old Nissan Maxima was perfect for the job. He insisted I lift the tree by myself even though I was only 5'8", and my dad was 6'3". I guess I got my height from my 5'3" mother. His excuse was that he was almost sixty and shouldn't be lifting anything. That was his excuse for everything these days.

"That's what I got two boys for," he always said.

I lifted the tree over my shoulder, and with a grunt, I tossed it on the roof. He just had to get a ten-foot tree. I looked over my shoulder to see him chuckling with his hands in his pockets. Once we had it tied down, we got in the car to go home.

"Why don't you ever have gas in your car?" he asked.

My gas light just clicked on as we pulled out of the lot. I rarely had over half a tank of gas. Gas prices were at their peak, and I was a struggling college student. At least, that was my excuse.

"Don't worry. I'll get some cash at the bank and stop for gas on my way to class tomorrow."

We got the tree home, put it in the stand with some water, and cut all the wire around it. Its branches exploded open as I cut the last piece of wire. We decided to wait until the next evening to decorate it so the tree had time to relax itself after being tied up for so long. That night, I went to bed preparing to go to class in the morning. The fall semester of my senior year of college was quickly coming to an end. We were spending these last few weeks preparing for finals. Unfortunately I would never make it to class the next morning.

I woke early Monday morning to some unusual commotion. I squinted at the clock, 6:30 a.m., an hour before my alarm was set to go off. I opened my bedroom door and looked down the hallway. Through my blurred vision, I could see light coming from the kitchen. Still half asleep, I walked down the hallway toward the kitchen, where I found my mom still dressed in her pajamas with her hair up in a messy bun. She was always the first one up in the morning, so I wasn't surprised to see her. For twenty years, she woke up at 5:00 a.m. to catch the early train to work in Manhattan. More recently, she worked part-time in the main office of my old high school. Her shift started at eight, and it was only a few blocks away. But she still woke up at five o'clock every morning. She couldn't help it. That was just what her body was used to after all those years commuting to the city.

She had her back turned to me as she leaned against the counter. She was on the phone. I could barely make out what she was saying, but I could tell she was crying. My brother was awake as well. He, on the other hand, could never wake up on time. Seeing him awake at this hour was unusual. I knew something was wrong. He sat at the kitchen table with his head buried in his hands. His greasy long brown hair hung down over his ears.

"What's going on?" I said.

My mom turned toward me suddenly with the phone still to her ear. Her face was flush, and her eyes were watery.

"I THINK YOUR FATHER'S DEAD!" she screamed at the top of her lungs.

Just hearing those words and seeing the expression on my mom's face was enough to seemingly knock the wind out of me. I wanted to respond, but I just couldn't. So many questions flooded my head at once I just froze there with my mouth open in shock, unable to formulate a sentence.

"He collapsed at work!" my mom continued. "They took him to Mercy Hospital in Queens. We have to leave right now!"

Could I be dreaming? Where the hell is Mercy Hospital? How do we get there? All questions I thought to myself as I scrambled to get myself together.

I had never driven to Queens before. My mom knew the area better than I since she grew up in Queens. There was no way she could drive in the condition that she was in. She was a nervous driver as it was. There was no way my little brother was going to be able to do that drive. I use the term *little brother* figuratively. While I got my height from my mom, he got his height from my dad at just over six feet tall. He only had his license for a few months, so it fell on me to drive us to the hospital.

"Kevin," I said, "look up the hospital's address so we know where the hell we're going."

I grabbed my keys and stormed out the front door. I made it to the base of the front porch when suddenly I realized my car didn't have any gas. There was no way we had time to stop to get some.

"Crap!" I said as I did a one-eighty and went back inside. "Kevin, give me the keys to your car. Mine's out of gas."

He grabbed his keys and tossed them to me.

"You figure out how to get there?" I asked.

"Yeah, I have it on my phone," he replied.

The three of us grabbed our coats, shoes, phones, etc. and hopped into my brother's car. It was another Nissan he inherited from my parents when they got the Cadillac. How he ended up with a car that was nearly ten years newer than mine, I couldn't tell you. I sat behind the wheel. My mom took the passenger's seat, and my brother sat in the back ready to help me navigate. When I started the car, I noticed that his car barely had more gas than mine.

You've got to be kidding me, I thought to myself.

It would have to do. I jammed the car in reverse and sped out of the driveway.

"Take the expressway," said Kevin, looking at the map on his phone.

I made my way to the Long Island Expressway as fast as I could, trying to avoid as many side streets as possible. Stop signs were optional. I didn't care too much about the rules of the road. My adrenaline was flowing. I hit turns hard. I braked hard when I needed to and accelerated as soon as I could. The tires were screeching, and I could feel the transmission slip from time to time. I was pushing the car hard. My car would never have been able to handle aggressive driving such as this. While I was driving, I was keeping a close eye on the fuel gauge.

When we finally merged onto the expressway, I was able to reach highway speeds. With not much to do but go straight for miles on end, question after question started to pop into my head. I leaned to my mom in the passenger seat.

"Wait, so who called you? Who were you speaking to on the phone earlier?" I asked.

"Larry," she replied in a broken voice.

"Larry? Retired Larry? How was he the one to call you?" My confusion only grew.

"I have no idea."

"No one from the bus depot contacted you?"

"No," she said. "I don't understand how that happened."

This didn't make any sense. How do you not inform someone's family first when something like this happens? How could Larry possibly find out before us?

"Okay, well, what did he say? Does he know what happened?"

"Uh…," my mom replied as she tried to recall exactly what was said over the phone. "He didn't know exactly what happened."

She was pretty shaken up and had a hard time gathering the details.

"The first thing he said was 'Diane, I hate to be the one to tell you this,' then went on to say that your father made it to work and collapsed at his desk. He was rushed to the hospital, and he said to get there as soon as we can. I knew, as soon as I saw his name come upon the caller ID, that something was wrong."

Larry was not the kind of person that would typically call the house in the early hours of the morning.

We raced on, fighting our way through the early morning traffic. I jumped from lane to lane—from the left lane to the center, back took the left, then center, then to the right as if I was in the final laps of the Daytona 500. I was laser focused on the road ahead, grasping tightly to the wheel with both hands. My mom held on tight to her door's handle. My brother, who was sitting in the backseat without a seat belt, was struggling to stay upright. The fuel gauge was hovering dangerously close to empty. Still we pressed on. This was no time to be gas conscious. This was truly a matter of life and death. Soon after we hit the expressway did my mom get a call on her cell phone. It was a number she didn't recognize.

"Hello?" she answered.

"Diane? Diane, my name's Johnny. I work with your husband. A few of us followed the ambulance to the hospital and were waiting outside the ER. Are you on your way? How far away are you?"

"We're on our way. We're…" She glanced out the window to get an idea of where we were. "We just passed Exit 30 on the expressway."

"Okay. We will wait outside for you. Meet us by the north entrance, okay? The *north* entrance. Don't worry about parking the car. There's a couple guys here. One of us will park it for you."

"Thank you so much, Johnny," replied my mom.

"Don't mention it," Johnny answered. "Describe your car so I know what I'm looking for when you pull up."

"We're in my son's car. It's a 2007 smoke-gray Nissan Altima with black wheels. I'll call you back when we're closer. Thank you again." She hung up.

Mere seconds after my mom hung up the phone did I notice a wall of red brake lights up ahead with just a few exits left to go. The traffic had come to an absolute standstill, and we were approaching fast. I took my foot off the gas, and we began to slow down.

My brother felt the car decelerating, and before I could depress the brake pedal, he exclaimed, "What are you doing? Why are you slowing down?"

My right arm jetted out over the dashboard, with my outstretched hand pointing toward the stopped traffic steadily approaching.

"You don't see that?" I replied.

"Use the shoulder! We need to keep going!" he snapped back at me like it was the obvious thing to do.

I hesitated, unclear at that moment what to do. My foot hovered over the brake pedal, and we were getting dangerously close to the vehicle in the right lane ahead of us.

"Brian…," my mom chimed in.

I was running out of time. I had to make a decision. My eyes darted to the open space on the side of the expressway. We were closing in fast!

"Brian!" my mom shouted nervously. "Slow. Down."

She leaned back in her seat. She braced herself against the dashboard. My brother was now leaning forward between the two front seats. I could feel his hot morning breath on my neck.

"Do it!" my brother shouted in my ear.

At the last possible second, I jerked the steering wheel to the right! The car swerved onto the shoulder, narrowly missing the car ahead of us by a couple of inches. The passenger-side mirror made a hiss as it briefly scraped the guardrail. I hit the accelerator once again, and we rushed past everyone in the right lane.

"Damn it, Brian! It doesn't do us any good if we show up there dead!" my mom said as she braced herself against any part of the car she could reach.

I didn't respond. I was laser focused on navigating between the vehicles to our left and the guardrail inches away from our right. Both my hands gripped the steering wheel tight. My knuckles were white from the pressure. Adrenaline was rushing through me.

"Our exit should be coming up," my brother said as he looked down at his phone again.

"This one coming up? Are you sure?" I questioned.

"Uh...," he hesitated.

"Are you sure?"

"Yes!" he answered. "Take it."

As the exit approached, the shoulder we had been riding in merged with the exit ramp. We bared right and coasted up the hill and onto a new parkway. I breathed a sigh of relief as this road wasn't nearly as congested and we could drive at full speed without worry. That sense of relief, however, was short-lived.

Soon after merging onto the parkway, something on the dashboard caught my attention. My eyes darted from the road down to the dashboard to see that the compass now read north. My eyes did a double take—from the dashboard, to the road, and back again. I knew this couldn't be correct. I didn't have much experience driving in this area, but I knew one thing. Queens was directly east of where we lived. There was no reason to travel north.

"Uh, why does the dashboard compass say we're headed north?" I announced.

For a moment, there was silence. Then my mom came to a terrible realization.

"Oh, no," she said, peering out the passenger-side window to read the signs we were passing. "This is the Whitestone Parkway."

"You mean as in the Whitestone Bridge?" I replied.

"Yes," she answered. "It's going to be coming up soon, and I don't think there's a way to exit the parkway before we reach it."

"Wait, are you saying we took the wrong exit?"

"Yes."

"Well, where does this go?"

My mom hesitated briefly. "The Bronx."

Through all this, my brother remained quiet in the back seat. He may very well have just made the biggest blunder of his entire life.

The Bronx? I thought to myself.

That was nowhere near where we needed to go, and there was no way to turn around. We were traveling away from my dad now instead of going toward him, all the while not knowing whether or not he was even still breathing. I normally was the calm person in the family, always able to keep my cool, but my emotions were reaching a boiling point. I couldn't contain them anymore.

"Damn it!" I shouted as I pounded on the steering wheel.

I was furious. I was mad that this all had to happen, mad at my brother for telling me to get off at the wrong exit, but also mad at myself for making such a dire mistake. I was the one behind the wheel, so in the end, it was my responsibility. I know now that there was no way I could have been prepared for such a journey, but at the time, I couldn't have been harder on myself.

"What do we do now?" I said, trying to regain my composure.

"I'll call Johnny back," my mom said. "Maybe he can help guide us back."

She reached for her phone, found the number from the most recent call, and hit redial. He answered right away. She put him on speaker.

"Johnny? Johnny, listen. We took the wrong exit. We are headed north on the Whitestone Parkway. We need you to help us find our way."

"Oh, shit," Johnny replied. "Did you cross the bridge yet?"

"No, but it's coming up. I can see it in the distance."

"Okay, listen. You're going to have to cross the bridge. As soon as you do, keep to the right and exit onto Route 278. Make sure you head west. That way you'll wrap around Queens and circle back toward Mercy Hospital. Once you're close enough, you'll see signs for Queens Boulevard. Take the exit south onto Queens Boulevard and follow signs to the hospital. It's only a few blocks from there. Call me if you need more help."

"Okay," my mom replied, "we'll give it a shot."

She hung up. On the other end of the call, Johnny relayed what was said on the phone to a couple of the guys that were still waiting at the hospital with him, all wearing their pale-blue bus driver uniforms and dark-blue winter jackets.

"They're headed toward the Whitestone," he said to the group as he put his phone back in his pocket. "They took the wrong exit."

Dave, another one of my dad's coworkers, spoke up, "You know what? I know a guy who works for the transit police. I'll call him. Hopefully someone can flag them down at the toll and turn them around." He dialed the number and held it up to his ear as it rang. He turned to Johnny. "You have a description of the car, right?"

"Yeah, it's a gray '07 Altima with black rims."

"Hey, Joe!" Dave said as his friend answered. "We got a situation here. There's a car headed north toward the Whitestone Bridge, and we need to turn it around. Don't worry about why. Trust me. It's a gray 2007 Nissan Altima. Have one of your troopers be on the lookout for it. Thanks, Joe. I owe you one."

It was too late. By the time Dave could get in touch with the toll plaza police, we had blown past it. My mom scrambled through her purse to find enough cash to get us through. We crossed the bridge and followed signs for Route 278. My brother said nothing for the past few miles. I wanted to yell at him, but I chose not to. I was angry with him, but I knew he was punishing himself enough. He didn't need me making remarks, so we all remained silent as we again headed west.

While I did find some relief in seeing the dashboard compass once again say west, I was faced with worry once again when the gas light chimed on. It seemed like the odds were stacked against us. We just had to pray that whatever gas we had left in the tank would get us to the hospital.

We somehow managed to navigate our way back to Queens. We were running on fumes, both literally, being short on gas, and figuratively, in regard to our nerves. As we approached the Mercy Hospital's north entrance, we could see two men still standing outside waiting for us. One was wearing his blue Triboro bus driver uniform and jacket while the other was in street clothes. When we got close, the one in uniform waved us down. We pulled up right to the emergency drop-off lane. We had finally made it. I had never been so relieved to step out of a car in all my life.

"Johnny?" my mom presumed, looking at the unfamiliar face.

"Yes, ma'am," he replied. "I'm sorry we had to meet under these circumstances."

You would think, by looking at him, that he should have retired long ago. His hair was almost entirely gray with coarse gray facial hair. He was skinny and had dark skin, clearly Italian, like most of the older guys who worked at the bus depot. He turned to me still standing outside the car with one hand on the roof and the other holding the driver's door.

"Give me the keys, son. I'll find a place to park it for you."

I tossed him the keys. He hopped inside, and we watched him quickly pull away to park the car in a nearby garage. For some reason, the hospital didn't have one of its own. The three of us turned and made our way onto the sidewalk. We then noticed the other gentlemen waiting to greet us outside the hospital entrance, wearing torn jeans, white T-shirt, and navy-blue hoodie.

"Billy!" my mother exclaimed.

Billy was an old childhood friend of my dad. They grew up on the same street back in Richmond Hill. They were both in their midtwenties when they started their training together as bus drivers for Triboro. My dad made a career out of it and, after fifteen years of driving, was promoted to dispatcher. Billy, on the other hand, knew driving a bus wasn't his true calling. After ten years or so, he left to join the NYPD. After a long career serving New York, he retired. He still lived in Richmond Hill with his wife, mere blocks from where he and my dad would play stickball in the street as kids.

He looked like a cop. He still had that mandatory buzz cut and a decent-size mustache. He was approaching sixty years old, same as my dad, so he had a good amount of gray on his head.

"What are you doing here?" my mom questioned.

"I heard what happened this morning. Word's already going around. Richie's my oldest friend," Billy said, starting to get choked up. "I knew I had to come down."

He gave my mom a hug, greeted my brother and me, then escorted us inside. My heart was beating out of my chest as we entered the hospital fearing the worst.

CHAPTER 2

HE WAS STILL ALIVE, BUT barely. A nurse had informed us that his heart still wasn't beating regularly and they were still working on him. They shoved us in a little shoebox of a waiting room down the hall in the meantime. The room maybe could fit four people comfortably—that is, if the fourth person sat on the floor. There were three cheap black chairs lined up against the wall. On the opposite side of the room, if you can call it that, was a misplaced cabinet and sink. The sink was old and dingy. The countertop was painted a dull gray, and the cabinets underneath were a faded mint green. The walls and moldings were painted to match. Atop the counter was a small coffee maker with burnt grounds caked to the bottom of the pot. It wasn't what most people would call a comforting environment.

Johnny came back from parking the car a few minutes after we sat down in the waiting room. He jogged the whole way back and was out of breath. He said the car was in an independently owned garage about a block away. He reached into his pocket and handed me the parking slip. I put it in my wallet for safekeeping.

"It's forty bucks to park there for the day," he said, trying to catch his breath. "Don't worry about it though. I took care of it."

"Oh, thank you," my mom replied. "I'll pay you back when I get the cash."

"I appreciate that. But it's not necessary."

"Johnny, you were there, right?" my mom asked, trying to get some answers. "Can you please just tell us what the hell happened? Someone has to."

Johnny exhaled deeply, put his hands in his pockets, and leaned against the doorway to the hall. We all braced ourselves. My mom, my brother, and I sat on the edge of our seats. Billy, who had been leaning against the counter, folded his arms and stared Johnny dead in the eye.

"Okay," Johnny proceeded. "Yes, I was there, but I didn't realize what had happened until I saw the ambulance pull up. I did, however, get as many details as I could from the guys who were around."

Johnny went on to tell us the story of the events that led us all here to this very moment.

*****

It started off as a normal morning. My dad and his partner, Lorenzo, were sitting in the dispatch office in the middle of the bus depot. Lorenzo was a heavyset Italian with stereotypical gelled-back hair and a pencil-thin mustache. Just after 6:00 a.m., their usual order of coffee and bagels was dropped off by the deli around the corner. My dad always got an everything bagel with a slab of butter wedged between the two halves. Looking back, that probably wasn't the smartest option. Overnight drivers were pulling their buses into the garage, and the morning drivers were just clocking in.

The depot where they worked was quite large. Most of the buses were parked indoors in a hangarlike building—three rows deep, twenty to thirty rows wide, depending on how many buses were on the road. The rest were forced to park outside in the elements, only to be brought inside for maintenance. Like most mass transit drivers, they got their routes and bus numbers assigned to them after clocking in. That's where my dad came in. He and the other dispatchers like Lorenzo had the job of assigning routes to every driver as well as monitoring each bus out in the field to make sure all the stops were completed in a timely fashion.

Like every morning, drivers were filing in, making their way to the dispatch window. My dad and the drivers would bullshit with each other as each route was being assigned, mess around, joke, and they would be on their way. A man by the name of Jerry Russo made his way to the dispatch window. He was short and muscular with a shaved head. He walked over to the window to find my dad on the phone, so he stood there patiently sipping his coffee. This was not his regular shift. He always worked in the late afternoon but was picking up a few extra shifts to help pay for his motorcycle that he was restoring. He had a faded-black Harley-Davidson from the early 1980s. He elongated the front suspension and installed a brand-new black leather seat and new chrome wheels. The engine still needed some work. It sputtered and popped as he rode. Everyone knew when he was coming by the sound of his exhaust. He was probably the only guy around still riding his bike to work with the cold December air moving in from the north. Not many people knew this about Jerry, but he was also a certified EMT. Little did he know that his training would be put to the test today.

Jerry sipped his morning coffee as he waited for my dad to give him his route. He wasn't used to coming in so early, so the coffee was extra strong. Lorenzo got up from his chair and left the room to go to the bathroom. Soon after, my dad, still on the phone, started to lean forward against his desk. He braced his forehead against the open palm of his free hand. Jerry turned his attention away from his coffee.

"Hey, Rich, you feeling okay?" Jerry said as he peered through the glass.

"I don't know. I don't feel right," my dad murmured.

He wasn't even acknowledging his associate on the other end of the phone line. His words began to slur. Jerry's concern grew.

"Rich! Rich, can you hear me?" Jerry exclaimed.

At that very moment, the phone fell from my father's grip and crashed onto the floor. Jerry's EMT training kicked in, and he immediately sprang into action. He raced around the dispatch window and busted through the door on the opposite side right as my dad began to fall out of his chair. He slid to his side where he was just able to catch my dad's head before it slammed against the concrete floor. His body was limp, and he wasn't breathing. My dad had no pulse. Jerry immediately started doing chest compressions when Lorenzo returned from his trip to the bathroom.

"Oh my God! What the hell happened?" he shouted in shock.

"Hurry, get the defibrillator!" Jerry responded.

Lorenzo grabbed the keys out of his pocket and unlocked the first aid cabinet where the defibrillator was stored. He swung the doors open but froze in disbelief.

"Lorenzo, let's go!" Jerry shouted.

"It's not in here…"

"What?"

"I said it's not in here!"

There was, in fact, an empty space in the first aid cabinet where the defibrillator was supposed to be stored. By now, the commotion caused a crowd to gather.

"There's one in the office upstairs!" someone announced.

A group ran up the stairs to retrieve it. All the while, Jerry was still on the floor trying to get my dad's heart beating again; but without a defibrillator, he was fighting a losing battle. Without the lifesaving device, his chances of survival were decreasing by the second. Multiple people called 911, including Lorenzo, who was a mess. He could barely hold his phone because he was shaking so much. He wanted to do more to help, but there wasn't much difference he could make without a defibrillator.

"I'm still not getting a pulse," he said. "We're going to lose him!"

Lorenzo wiped cold sweat from his forehead. His face turned pale. He was watching the man he had been working with every day for years slowly slip away. Finally two drivers came charging to the room with the nearest defibrillator they could find. Jerry quickly grabbed it from them. He violently ripped open my dad's shirt and placed the paddles on his chest.

"Clear!" Jerry announced.

He checked for a pulse. Nothing. So he tried again.

"Clear!"

Jerry checked for a pulse once more. He felt one, but it was faint and sporadic. Just then, flashing red and blue lights shined through the windows. The ambulance arrived, and the hospital EMTs took over. At 6'3", and weighing nearly 250 pounds, it took five men to lift his limp body onto the stretcher.

*****

"They loaded him into the back of the ambulance and took off," Johnny wrapped up. "I felt like I couldn't just sit there or go back to work." You could see this had taken a toll on him. "So I decided to follow the ambulance."

We were all taken aback by this information, desperately trying to process it all. My brother was pale, and my mom had tears running down her face.

"Wait," said my brother, "how did you get my mom's cell phone number?"

Johnny cocked his head, seemingly puzzled by the question. "Oh, I called Larry and told him what happened. I asked for a way to reach Richie's family, so he gave me your mother's number."

I turned toward my mom. "I guess that explains how Larry ended up being the one who broke the news."

"You were never contacted by the company?" Johnny asked.

"Nope," my mom replied.

"Jesus," Johnny said, shaking his head. He looked down at his watch. "I better get going. They are probably going to make me fill out a report or some bullshit like that. I just wanted to make sure you guys got here okay."

"I'll find some way to pay you back for the garage money," said my mom.

Johnny waved his hand at her and shook his head. "No, no. Don't worry about that. Just worry about getting your husband back to work. He still owes me lunch," Johnny joked as he attempted to lighten the mood.

We said our goodbyes, and he walked off.

Time passed slowly. We all remained quiet, sitting in that room for what felt like an eternity. Billy was off pacing up and down the hall. The scene of me waking up to my mom screaming was playing in my head on repeat.

I think your father's dead! I think your father's dead! I think your father's dead!

It went through my mind over and over, digging deeper and deeper into my subconscious. I leaned forward and rubbed my eyes in an attempt to break the cycle in my mind, but it didn't work. The walls were closing in. It felt like the room was suffocating me. I needed some air, so I walked into the hall. My legs felt so weak I had to brace myself against the wall. I closed my eyes and took a deep breath.

I reopened my eyes to see a dark figure down the hall walking toward us. Even from far away, you could tell he was a giant. He was walking with a purpose straight for me. He was dressed in black from head to toe—black suit, long black coat, and black fedora. Just the sight of him made my heart rate spike. When you see a man dressed in all black walking away from an emergency room, your mind starts jumping to conclusions.

He's an undertaker or the coroner. He must be. He's coming to break the news. My dad is gone. That's it. He's gone.

The man came closer and closer. I turned pale and started to quiver, unable to control my nerves. He finally walked up to me. He was an older man with a long gray beard.

"Excuse me. I'm looking for the family of Richard Pellegrino," he said with a thick Russian accent, as if his presence wasn't intimidating enough.

"That's us," I cautiously replied. "I'm his oldest son."

My mom and brother overheard this man and me talking and stepped into the hallway. My mom looked him up and down. I think the sight of this man had the same effect on her as it did on me, judging by the look of concern painted on her face.

"I'm Richard's wife," she said quietly. "Who might you be?"

"Hello, Mrs. Pellegrino. My name is Ivan Draganov," he replied with an outstretched hand.

My mom shook his hand.

"I am a liaison for the Triboro Bus Company. I was sent here on behalf of their corporate office when they heard about what happened. I am so sorry that you and your family are being put through this. If there is anything I can do to make this time easier for you, you let me know. If you need his pension or 401(k) information, I can get those records for you as well so you can start to get his affairs in order."

The nerve of this guy. First, who walks into an ER waiting room dressed in black from head to toe? He nearly gave us all heart attacks! Second, he was speaking as if my dad was already dead. *Get his affairs in order*? Was he next going to offer to help us plan my dad's funeral? This guy really got my brother heated. He stepped right up to Mr. Draganov.

"Who the hell do you think you are?" he exclaimed.

"Kevin," said my mom.

She reached to grab his shoulder in an attempt to reel him in, but he shrugged her away.

"Don't you dare try to put my dad in an early grave!"

"I'm sorry to be so blunt," Mr. Draganov responded calmly as he kept his attention toward my mom. "But from the information I have gathered, your husband's situation is dire. I suggest you prepare yourselves for the worst."

He spoke to us with little compassion, drawing no attention to the fearful expressions on our faces. His response to my brother's little outburst seemed rehearsed, robotic like. It didn't faze him one bit. I'm assuming he was used to dealing with employee's families in times of crisis.

"Look," my mom spoke up, "now is the wrong time. We haven't even spoken to a doctor yet. Tell you what. If we need you, we'll get in touch with you."

He gave a quick nod, reached into his coat pocket, and pulled out a business card.

"Very well. Let me give you this."

"Fine," my mom said as she snatched the card from his hand.

Mr. Draganov looked at all of us one last time, tipped his cap, gave us all a cheap smile, turned around, and walked away.

"Asshole," my brother muttered under his breath as we reluctantly shuffled back into the waiting room.

We took our seats. My mom looked down at the business card still in her hand. A look of frustration and agony poured from her face. She couldn't look at it anymore, so she aggressively jammed it in her purse. We again sat quietly, each one of us alone with our thoughts. That is when Billy strolled back in.

"Anyone spoken to you guys yet?" he said.

"No, not yet," I replied.

Billy threw his head back and sighed in frustration. I was getting tired of playing the waiting game. I took out my phone to see what time it was, eleven thirty. We had been sitting there for hours. At that moment, I realized this was the first time since this whole ordeal began that I had taken my phone out of my pocket. I unlocked the screen to find four unanswered texts and two missed calls from my girlfriend, Nicole. I silence my phone when I go to bed so I'm not awakened by notifications during the night. I must have never thought to turn the ringer back on.

Nicole was my everything. We were high school sweethearts. We met just a week before senior prom. After one date, I asked her to prom, and the rest was history. She was everything I was looking for—short, Italian like me, and with silky long brown hair and big brown eyes. Her skin was fair, and her smile could light up a room. She was one of the most kind and thoughtful people I had ever met.

She must have been worried. I always shoot her a good-morning text when I wake up. We also usually call each other on our way to class in the morning. She went to a community college working toward her dream of becoming a teacher. Since our fall semesters were coming to a close, we knew each other's schedules by heart. It was extremely unlike me to not contact her so late in the morning. While I can honestly say I wasn't aware of her many attempts to reach me until that very moment, truth be told, I was avoiding calling her myself.

I kept thinking to myself, *What do I say? Should I wait? She'll just worry.*

Well, so much for that. My lack of communication worried her all the same. Perhaps I just didn't want to say what was going on out loud. That would make it seem all too real. I came to the conclusion that it wouldn't be right to keep her in the dark any longer. I looked down nervously at my phone.

My mom noticed this; and as if she could read my mind, she said, "Call her."

I looked up and gave her a nod. I whipped my cheek and stepped into the hallway to call Nicole. It rang slowly two or three times before she answered.

"Babe?" I said.

"Hey! Where have you been? I've been trying to get a hold of you!"

"Yeah, uh, I know. Sorry."

She heard my broken voice and said, "What's wrong?"

I started to tear up. My voice started to crack.

"It's my dad," I replied. "He was rushed to the hospital this morning. It sounds like he had a heart attack!"

"What? Oh my God!" she shouted. "Are you okay?"

"I honestly don't know," I answered, holding back my tears.

She began to tear up also. I could hear her start to sob over the phone. Although we had only been dating for a few short years, my dad and Nicole had become very close. He was like a second father to her. She had a hard time handling situations like this. She especially hated the idea of doctors and hospitals. Who could blame her? I took a deep breath so I could continue.

"We're at the hospital now. Me, Kevin, and Mom. He's still in the ER."

"Which hospital are you at?"

"Mercy Hospital. It's in Queens."

"Why did they send him there?"

"Well, I guess it was closest to his job."

"Oh, right, of course. Do you need me to drive out to you?"

"No, no. I appreciate it, babe, but I don't want you to make that drive by yourself. I'll let you know if you need to. Right now, we honestly don't know anything."

"Are you sure? I'd do it in a heartbeat!"

I knew she would. She would do anything for me, and I for her. Although I wanted nothing more than to put my arms around her, I didn't think her car could make it this far. Her '97 Chevy Cavalier was in such terrible condition. It barely made it down the driveway, let alone to Queens. She prayed every morning for the thing to start. Not only that, but I honestly didn't want her to see me like this. I don't know if it was embarrassment or some misplaced sense of masculinity, but I was trying to avoid the situation of me breaking down in front of her.

"I know you would, babe," I replied. "I love you so much."

"I know. I love you too."

"Let me go. I'll text you when we hear something."

"Okay. Bye, babe."

"Bye." I hung up and walked into the room.

All three of them looked up at me. Billy, who had been occupying my seat, leaned forward to get up. I shook my hand in his direction.

"Sit, sit. I'm fine standing," I said to him.

He sat back in the chair once again.

I leaned against the counter and crossed my arms. I was tired of waiting in limbo. Any longer, and I would chase down any nurse or doctor I could find and demand answers. Just as my frustration was reaching its tipping point, a nurse dressed in pink scrubs holding a clipboard appeared in the doorway. She was still wearing a surgical mask. We all stood up out of our chairs. We all towered over her, even my mom. The nurse couldn't have been more than five feet tall. Her shiny blond hair was tied up in a messy bun. She had hazel-green eyes, but they were bloodshot. She looked exhausted. It must have been a long morning for her as well. She pulled down her mask before she addressed us.

"Pellegrino?" she said.

My mom was quick to reply. "Is he okay? Where is he? What's going on?"

The nurse spoke calmly, "He's still in the ER, but they just got him stable enough to move. In a few minutes, they are going to take him to the cardiac intensive care unit. It appears your husband suffered some kind of cardiac event which caused his heart to stop beating."

"What do you mean cardiac event?" Billy interrupted.

"I'm sorry, but I don't have all the details," replied the nurse. "Once you are up in the ICU, the doctor will be able to further answer your questions. Why don't you all go up there now? Richard will be assigned a room shortly."

"Where is the ICU?" I asked.

"On the seventh floor, toward the north side of the building. I'll show you to the elevator."

So just like that, she escorted us out of that miniature waiting area and down the hall to the elevator. Before we reached the elevator, we had to pass the emergency room. Through the glass, I got the first glance of my dad's unconscious body. Time seemed to slow down more and more with each step. His face was pale and lifeless. A breathing tube was down his throat, and there was bile running down his cheek. As he breathed, his chest was violently and sporadically expanding and contracting. It seemed unnatural, machinelike. It freaked me out. I reached forward and grabbed the nurse by the shoulder.

"Hey, why is he breathing like that?"

She turned her upper body toward me but never broke her stride. "That's due to the ventilator we put him on. It's trying to supply him with a steady flow of oxygen. The reason his chest is expanding like that is because his body is working against it."

In true medical fashion, it was an explanation that led to more questions than answers. I saved my follow-up questions for the doctor as the nurse suggested earlier. We arrived at the elevator and walked on, leaving the nurse to her work. We soon arrived on the seventh floor. My mom briskly approached the nurses' counter in the cardiac wing of the ICU.

"Hello. Did Richard Pellegrino receive a room yet?"

The nurse sitting behind the counter, a heavyset Jamaican woman, quickly tapped on her keyboard. "Um, no, but he'll be on his way up soon. Please have a seat in the visitors' area, and I will come get you when he's set up in his room."

My mom exhaled deeply with exhaustion. Leaning against the counter with her head down, she replied, "Okay. Thank you."

She sounded defeated. This day had defeated us all, and it was barely noon. We slowly made our way to the next waiting area. At least, it was empty. The last thing we needed was to share a room with other grieving families.

This room was far bigger than the last with large cushioned chairs, floor-to-ceiling windows, and open floor space. There were two vending machines against the wall, one food and one beverage. There was a small counter next to them with a large coffeemaker, an assortment of roasts, and sugar packets. Having a window to look out of was a good change of pace. My brother leaned his shoulder against the glass and peered into the distance. There wasn't much to look at. Outside the window was a dismal scene of dirty rooftops atop decrepit brick buildings. Steam rising from the chimneys filled the horizon with haze. Car horns sounded off on the streets below.

Our stay in this room was far shorter than the last. It must not have been ten minutes before a nurse greeted us. She explained that my dad was in room 12A. It was all the way at the end of the hall, last room on the left. The scene as we walked down the hall was bleak. We were forced to walk past all the other rooms in the cardiac ICU, forced to walk past all the patients barely clinging to life and past all their grieving loved ones. Their cries filled the hallway like an echo chamber. It was truly like walking down death row. Even at our brisk pace, the hallway seemed to be never ending. We finally reached the end of the hallway. At its very end was a window with a view of the Manhattan skyline.

We slowed down as we approached 12A, afraid of what we might see. We entered cautiously. My dad, the sole occupant, lied unconscious in the middle of the room. They had cleaned the bile from his face and neck. The breathing tube was still down his throat, but at first glance, it seemed that his breathing had somewhat normalized. There were so many wires and tubes connected to him. Machines beeped and hummed. It was enough to drive anyone insane. We slowly circled the bed in which he lay—my brother and I on his right, Billy by his feet, and my mom on his left. She took his hand in hers and held it tight. Tears ran down her face. It was unbearable. I felt I had to be strong for my mom. I looked over to my brother who was barely keeping it together. What do you do? What do you say in a moment like this?

My mom moved in closer and gently spoke in his ear.

"Richard?" My mom sniffled. "Richard, I'm here. The boys are here. Billy's here too. Can you hear me?"

We all stared at him for a moment, expecting some kind of response. There was nothing.

"Richard, you're okay. You're going to be okay," my mom continued. Her face tensed. "Damn it, Richard, answer me!" she seethed.

Suddenly an unfamiliar voice entered the room. "I'm afraid he can't."

We all spun toward the voice's direction to see a doctor dressed in his white coat standing in the doorway. He stepped forward.

"Mrs. Pellegrino? I'm Dr. Peterson. We need to talk."

CHAPTER 3

DR. PETERSON WAS A TALL, heavyset man with a pink complexion. He was almost completely bald. I would estimate he was in his late fifties. As head cardiac specialist for the entire intensive care unit, he oversaw the most challenging cases. With his experience, he was the guy you wanted looking over a loved one in crisis.

My mom stepped toward him.

"Doctor, I'm his wife, Diane. Please tell me he is going to be okay!"

"Come, let's talk in another room where it's more private. Follow me," the doctor said.

So we all started for the door, Billy included. The doctor noticed Billy joining us.

"I'm sorry, but it's usually best if I just speak to the patient's family during times like this," Dr. Peterson told Billy.

"I'm his brother," Billy swiftly replied.

Of course, he wasn't, but the doctor wasn't about to question it. So he agreed to have Billy join us. I glanced over at Billy and contemplated what he said. They were around the same age and close in height. Their mustaches were almost identical. Both had that distinctive New York accent. I guess I could see him and my dad being brothers.

We gathered in an empty room right next door to my dad's room, number 11A. The bed was freshly made with white linen untouched by any patient. The room was dark and quiet compared to my dad's. The only light came from the dreary, overcast day on the other side of the window. We filed in. My mom and Kevin sat on the edge of the bed. Billy and I preferred to stand. The doctor closed the door behind us.

"Okay," said Dr. Peterson as he took a deep breath, "here's what we know. Your husband went into cardiac arrest. That much is obvious. The question now is what exactly happened within the confines of his heart to cause it. When most people hear the term *cardiac arrest*, they immediately think heart attack. Based on what information I have gathered, I don't think that's the case. A heart attack, while devastating, comes with some kind of warning, chest pain, shortness of breath, etc. In Richard's case, his heart just stopped beating out of nowhere, and he dropped to the floor."

He paused briefly to let that first bit of information sink in. Then he continued, "Now that he is stable, we can run tests to see what caused that to happen."

"But if he's stable, like you say, why is he unconscious and on a ventilator?" I said.

"Here lies the concern," Dr. Peterson continued. "There are conflicting reports about how long your father's heart wasn't beating on its own. Depending on who we spoke to—whether it be his coworkers, the EMTs, or the emergency room staff—they all had different timeframes. Some said five minutes. Some said ten minutes, and…I have even heard thirty minutes. Please understand that, when the heart isn't beating or is beating irregularly for a long period of time, the brain doesn't receive a steady flow of oxygen-rich blood. When deprived of oxygen for a long enough period of time, brain cells begin to die off."

"Oh my God," said my mom. "You're talking about brain damage."

Not wanting to get ahead of himself, the doctor rolled on, "Imagine a brain. The outermost regions are what we consider 'newer' brain tissue, evolutionarily speaking. Those regions house things like personality traits, memory, fine motor skills, and the five senses. The deeper you go into the brain, the older and more primal the sections of the brain become. These are responsible for things like instinct, spinal cord function, and the brain's ability to send signals to the heart and lungs, to name a few."

Billy chimed in, "So what kind of damage can we expect here, Doc?"

Dr. Peterson paused briefly. "Well, it is unclear. Again, we are not sure how long his brain went without oxygen. That is why we have put him in a medically induced coma. In addition, we placed ice packs around his body to reduce the rate of cellular degradation. Our goal is to help his body and mind recover the best they can. The reason for the ventilator is we are not sure at this moment that he can breathe on his own."

"Wait, you said medically induced coma?" asked my brother.

"Yes," Dr. Peterson replied.

"So then can't he just pull out of it?"

"Not on his own. In a few days, we will slowly wean him off the drugs and test his cognitive response level."

"Doctor, please tell us what we can expect," said my mom.

"There are a few scenarios I can lay out for you. Yes, there is a slight chance that he wakes up perfectly normal. More likely is he wakes up with an unknown number of mental defects or disabilities. It's possible he may wake up only to be a vegetable. Unfortunately, however, based on all information given, I would have to say it is more likely that he never wakes up at all."

My mom started to cry again. Dr. Peterson stepped forward and put his hand on her shoulder.

"I'm sorry. I never like giving news like this. All you can do for him right now is pray. If I were you, however, I would prepare for any outcome no matter how grim. If you were to ask me, I suggest that you get his affairs in order."

There it was again. Get his affairs in order. Hearing that was like having the final knife plunged through our chests and into our hearts. Words can't describe the despair we all felt as we hugged each other. There didn't seem to be any hope.

"I'm sorry. I'll give you all some privacy," said Dr. Peterson. Just as he was about to step out of the room, he stopped, braced his hand against the door-frame, and looked back at us over his shoulder. "You can sit with him as long as you need."

He left us to continue on with his work.

There were many more cases on that floor to attend to. None of that mattered to us of course. The only thing on our minds was that man lying coma-tose in the next room, the leader of our family and my mom's rock for nearly thirty years.

With my brother at one side and me on the other, we walked my mom out of that empty room and back into my dad's, all the while having tears run down our faces. We hovered over him once again. He was so close, but at the same time, he seemed to be pulling farther away. At least, he seemed peaceful. I wondered what he was thinking, if anything. Could he hear us?

I recalled the great debate over whether or not people in comas can hear what goes on around them. I figured what the hell. I thought it would be good for him to hear our voices. I struggled to find some-thing to say. My mouth opened, but nothing came out. So I paused, took a second to sift through my thoughts, and tried again.

"Hi…Dad." The words barely came out. I had to push them past my vocal cords. "It's Brian. I drove all the way here, my first time driving to Queens. Not a fan. Ha-ha."

My brother decided to say something as well. He leaned in close and spoke quietly, "Hey, Pop."

He tried to continue, but it was too much for him. So he stepped out of the room. I reached over the bed to try to grab him, but he was gone in a hurry. Billy put his hand on my shoulder.

"Let him go," he said.

He was right. There was nothing I or my mom could say or do to make him feel better. It was best to just let him be.

Some time had passed, and tears led to numbness. By this time, we found our selected seats around the room. My brother had made his way back and was sitting on the floor, leaning against the wall opposite all the equipment. My mom pulled up a chair directly to the left side of my dad's bed. I took to the chair in the far corner of the room, and Billy took a seat on the windowsill. He looked down at his watch.

"Uh, I better get going," he said. "I have to get home to take the dog out."

"EDDIE!" the rest of us shouted simultaneously.

Eddie was our six-year-old Labrador retriever. We ran out of the house so quickly that we forgot about him. This was the first time during this whole ordeal that anyone had thought of him. I know Eddie is an odd name for a dog, but that's the name I came up with six years ago. I'm not sure where it came from, but it stuck.

"Oh my God," my mom said, "that poor thing. He's been alone all day. He must be starving."

"Did you take him out this morning?" I asked.

"Yeah, right before I got the call. But I didn't feed him."

"Oh, he'll be fine," Billy chimed in.

"Waiting for his daddy to come home…," I said, tearing up again.

As soon as my dad got up for work in the morning, Eddie would hop up and take his place on the bed. During the day, he would lie on the couch in the living room and stare out of the front window until my dad came home. The only thing that would get him off that couch was to eat or to go outside. With everyone out of the house, you could bet that was where he was, waiting patiently, most likely sleeping the day away in blissful ignorance. He was probably snoring. I could imagine him dreaming. We could always tell when he was dreaming because his feet would twitch. We always liked to guess what he was dreaming about. Perhaps he was chasing a squirrel.

Eddie was just under one hundred pounds by the time he was fully grown. Despite his size, he retained that puppylike energy. That was why, even at six years of age, we referred to him as "pup-ish." He was far from his days as a puppy but still acted like one. He was a ninety-pound ball of energy. He could take you out at the knee if you weren't careful while he was running around in the backyard. Like other yellow Labs, he had very light fur but with unique markings. His ears and the tip of his tail were golden brown, and he had a white strip going down his spine.

"I can't believe we forgot about him," said Kevin.

"Don't beat yourself up," replied Billy. "You've been through a lot today. You can allow yourself to forget a few things along the way."

He put on his hoodie and got ready to leave.

"Thank you for coming, Billy. It means a lot," said my mom.

"Of course, he's one of my oldest friends," Billy replied. He kneeled by my dad's side and laid his hand on his left arm. "Hey, you better wake up soon. You're driving everyone crazy, especially your wife."

Billy stood up and gave my mom a hug.

"Give Maria my best."

"You got it. Take care of her, boys," he said to me and my brother.

We both nodded as he turned to go home.

We sat in silence for hours. We didn't speak much. Each of us just sat in our respective cones of despair. My mom stepped out of the room from time to time calling loved ones, informing them of what had happened—her sister, my dad's brother, and his sister. Nurses would walk in periodically to check on him. His vitals remained constant. The many machines and sensors beeped and hummed. After a while, the noise just faded away. I barely heard it anymore. My eyes focused on the monitor displaying his vitals. I watched his heartbeat and blood pressure fluctuate over time. I wouldn't know if the numbers I was reading were good or bad. I watched to make sure he still had a heartbeat. I looked out the window to a sunset peeking through the clouds.

I cleared my throat and spoke up, "It's getting late. Traffic is going to get bad soon."

My voice was broken and lifeless to the point where it shook me a little bit.

"Yeah, you're right," said my mom, looking at the clock. "I guess we should go home."

"Not yet," Kevin said.

"What about Eddie?" my mom asked.

I stood up out of my chair for the first time in hours.

"She's right," I said to Kevin. "We'll come back first thing in the morning."

"Okay," Kevin said reluctantly.

We put on our coats and prepared to head out.

"Bye, Richard," my mom said to my dad. "We are going to go now. We got to go take care of Eddie. We'll be back in the morning." She then kissed his forehead.

"Bye, Dad. Love you," said Kevin.

I said the same. I tried to put my arms around my dad to give him a hug, but there were so many wires in the way. I was afraid of unplugging something, so I backed off.

We made our way down to the hospital's ground floor. As we walked outside, I took the parking ticket out of my wallet. The address was on the back.

"It's directly across from here," I said, looking at the street signs over the intersection in front of us.

We crossed the street and walked for about two blocks before we found it. It was an underground parking structure beneath an apartment building. The only way down was to walk down the steep drive ramp from the street. Carefully we made our way down, my brother ahead of me and my mom.

"We need to find the nearest gas station possible. There's probably nothing but fumes in the tank," I said.

Kevin took his phone out of his pocket. "I'll look one up."

"No, I'll do it," I replied.

Kevin stopped and turned, staring me down. "Why?"

I kept walking down the ramp until we were face-to-face. The incline put us face-to-face.

"Because I've seen how well you navigate," I said sarcastically, alluding to what had happened on the drive there.

"I was waiting for you to fucking bring that up!" he yelled.

"Yeah! Judging by the shit you pulled on the expressway, if you were in charge of finding a gas station, we would end up somewhere in fuckin' Jersey!"

"It was a mistake!" Kevin shouted. His voice echoed through the garage.

"The only mistake was trusting you to tell me where to go!"

Kevin was furious. His face turned beet red. He pushed me, but the slope of the ramp worked to my advantage. My heels just dug into the hill while

Kevin lost his balance and stumbled a bit, taking him a few steps down. My mom stepped in between us.

"Enough!" she shouted. "I am not in the mood for this shit! What's done is done! Now just get me the fuck home!"

We had never heard our mom curse like that before. It was extremely unnerving. We apologized and headed for the ticket office. A valet drove the car around. I took the keys from him, and we drove up the ramp and out. I hope he wasn't expecting a tip. There was a gas station a few blocks away on the corner. We pulled in. I filled up, and we headed home. By now, it was dark, and the evening rush-hour traffic had set in. It must have taken us an hour and a half to get home.

I pulled the car into the driveway. The house was dark. The only light came from the lamp over the front porch. Through the limited yellow light, I could just make out Eddie by the front window just as expected. He was fast asleep, resting his head on the armrest of the couch. I slammed the car door shut, and he awoke with a few barks before he realized it was us.

He greeted us as we walked in with his usual excitement and enthusiasm. He pushed toward us so hard we had to nudge him back to get through the doorway. His tail wagged so fast it created a breeze. We flipped on all the lights and combed through the house for any signs of him misbehaving or him having an accident in the house. It was all clear. He was a good boy all day. We all settled in the kitchen. My mom dropped her bag off on the table. I threw my jacket over a chair. Eddie came trotting in, holding his empty food bowl in his mouth, wagging his tail, and stomping ferociously. His hunger had distracted him from the fact that my dad wasn't with us. He was usually the first one home and was the one who fed him in the afternoon.

"You poor thing," said my mom, "you must be starving."

She grabbed the bowl out of his mouth and filled it up. He certainly was starving. He scarfed the food down in seconds without even chewing. He then lapped up some water and plopped on the floor with a full belly. This sparked the realization that I hadn't eaten all day. None of us had. Yet I wasn't hungry. I just felt empty, the same familiar emptiness I had been feeling all day.

We didn't speak. We didn't put on the television. We didn't answer the phone. We put distance between each other. My mom sat at the kitchen table. I sat alone in the living room, and my brother was God knows where. I sat in darkness. The only light on in the house was the eerie glow coming from the kitchen. With its help, I could make out the bare evergreen tree standing in front of me. Can you truly call it a Christmas tree if it's not decorated?

Bare it would remain. My dad promised we would all decorate it together—as a family. Not a single light or ornament would go on that tree until my dad came home. We were going to do it together or not at all.

CHAPTER 4

NONE OF US SLEPT THAT night. I just lay in bed staring up at the ceiling. The glow from the headlights of the occasional passing car would peer through the blinds. Lying there alone with my thoughts, I started to picture life without my dad. There was so much I wanted him around for and so much he still had to teach me. My eyes welled up as I fought to fall asleep. I tossed and turned. I clenched my pillow. I rubbed my eyes in an attempt to fight off the negative images. I looked at the clock every so often. Time was moving so slow. Finally I saw sunlight shining through my window. With the sun on the rise, I figured it was time to pull myself out of bed.

I made sure to call out of work. I worked part-time as a mechanic at a local auto repair shop to put myself through college. It was owned by an old married couple, Paul and Laura Morris. They had been together for decades and owned the shop for nearly as long. Paul did the majority of the repairs while Laura worked the front desk and did paperwork. They hired me after their son, Chris, joined the military. They were shorthanded, so they took a chance on this inexperienced kid barely out of high school. True, I didn't have much experience. But I was eager to learn, so Paul took me under his wing. They were really good to me. They let me work around my school schedule, and when I told them about my dad, they insisted I take all the time I need. My mom and Kevin didn't have an issue with work either. My brother was unemployed, so no problem there. My mom only worked a few days a week.

Once I fed Eddie and took him out, we hit the road. We left as early as possible to avoid the traffic. We took my brother's car again. With a full tank of gas, I drove like the morning before. Given the circumstances, there was a lot less pressure on this drive to the hospital compared to the last. I took my time, went the speed limit, rolled with the traffic, and found the correct exit off the expressway. Taking the proper route cut our travel time down a lot even with light morning traffic.

Parking was still a challenge. We managed to find a spot on the street a few blocks away from the hospital. We entered through the main entrance rather than the emergency room entrance the previous day. We needed to get visitors' passes. But because we were family, we just needed one, and we could use it every day. Nonfamily members had to sign in with every visit. We entered my dad's room in the ICU to find that not much had changed. He was still stable. That was about the only good news. We greeted him as we walked in to inform him that we were there.

We made ourselves at home. My mom went to go hunt down a nurse for any updates regarding his condition. She came back a few moments later after speaking with one of the nurses down the hall.

"His vitals were stable all night. No changes," my mom reported.

It could be worse, I thought to myself.

I tried to be optimistic. I was desperately trying to keep the dark and dismal thoughts of a future without my father out of my head. It was a new day, and the sun was shining. Perhaps there was some good news in store for us. Perhaps I was fooling myself. With not much else to do but loiter around the room, I walked into the hallway and gazed out the window at its very end. It would be the first of many trips to that window. As I leaned against the windowsill on this clear and sunny morning, I could see the Manhattan skyline perfectly. The buildings shimmered in the morning sun. It truly was a beautiful sight.

Across the hall in room 12B lay an elderly Hispanic woman surrounded by loved ones. She was barely conscious with not much movement. Her hair was gray and frayed. Her skin was like leather, and her eyes were sunken in. She looked so thin and frail. She must have been at least eighty years old. Her many children and grandchildren filled all available space around her, mostly talking among themselves. A middle-aged woman, possibly her oldest daughter, knelt beside her bed and whispered to her in Spanish. Occasionally the elderly woman would turn her head, try to speak, or attempt to raise an arm, anything to respond. I tried not to eavesdrop, so I retreated back to our room to give that family some privacy.

An hour passed with nothing but the monitors' various beeps to keep us company. Suddenly a familiar face emerged. Dr. Peterson walked in with a nurse and a technician in tow.

"Good morning, Pellegrino family," he said.

"Hello, Doctor. How are you?" my mom replied.

"I'm well. I hope you don't mind, but we're going to steal him for a bit so we can run some tests on his heart. I'm hoping we can get some clear answers today as to what caused this whole mess."

"Absolutely. Do whatever you can."

With that, the nurse and technician released the brakes from my dad's bed and carefully wheeled him out the door. What an amazing rig they had him in. All the IVs and monitors latched onto the sides, and it glided down the hall as one. In its place left an empty space in the middle of the room. With nothing tying us to the room for the moment, we decided to find the cafeteria and grab something to eat. I was starving. We hadn't eaten since Sunday evening. It's true what they say about hospital food: dry, tasteless, and stale; and it wasn't cheap.

We took the elevator back up to the seventh floor. As we walked down the hall, we approached the nurses' desk to see Dr. Peterson conversing with a nurse. He spotted us walking toward him and flagged us down.

"I'm glad I caught you guys," he said. "Come with me. I want to share with you what we found."

So we followed him back into our room in which my dad was once again occupying.

"So we performed a multitude of tests, an echo-cardiogram—otherwise known as an EKG—cardiac stress test, chest x-ray, bloodwork, etc. The good news is his arteries are clear. His cholesterol is surprisingly low for his age, but he does have high blood pressure."

"We knew that," my mom interrupted. "Do you think that was a contributing factor?"

"No, at least not entirely. We found a little bit of an arrhythmia in his heartbeat while performing the EKG."

"Arrhythmia?" Kevin asked.

"An irregular or inconsistent heartbeat. An arrhythmia was our first clue. The combination of the chest x-ray and the stress test helped us realize that the walls of the lower chambers of Richard's heart are unusually thick. This condition is known as hypertrophic cardiomyopathy or HOCM. When this occurs, the inner walls of the heart's lower chambers can make contact with each other when pumping blood. This causes an irregular heartbeat. In rare cases, this contact can cause the electrical signals from the brain to short out, which causes the heart to just stop beating. A jolt from a defibrillator is usually enough to jumpstart a person's heart once this occurs."

"Oh my God," said my mom.

"The combination of this HOCM, high blood pressure, stress, and age caused Richard's heart to shut down during one of these arrhythmias."

"That's a lot to wrap my head around," my mom said, rubbing her forehead. "I'm going to sit down. This is too much."

"Well, there is more that I feel you must know. This condition is something most patients are born with, and it can be hereditary, particularly"—he paused and looked toward my brother and I—"in the male side of the family."

"Are you saying my boys could have this condition?" my mom feared.

"It is very possible, but at their age, they're not in any immediate danger," the doctor assured us. "I would, however, suggest they both get tested sooner rather than later."

Could I have this affliction as well? Lying dormant in my chest waiting to strike at any moment? It pained me to think that I could be living with this heart defect for the rest of my life, never truly knowing when my time was going to be up. Suddenly I came to a realization.

"Wait a minute! Grandpa!" I proclaimed.

"What about him?" my mom asked.

"Don't you remember Dad telling the story of how he died?"

My grandfather Romeo, my dad's father, died in his fifties, long before my parents ever met. My dad said that he died suddenly of unknown causes. He was walking down the stairs one day in my grandparents' Queens home and quite literally "just dropped dead." He was dead before he hit the landing. This came as an extreme shock to the family. Aside from having a hearty Italian diet, he was in good shape and seemed healthy.

"Oh my God, you are right!" my mom said. She turned back to the doctor. "My father-in-law died suddenly when he was around my husband's age. His heart just stopped one day at home. They said back then that the cause was unknown, but they probably didn't know better back then. You think it's possible he had this…HOCM as well?"

"It is very possible," said Dr. Peterson. "Even if he was suspected of having this condition, the technology of the time wouldn't have been able to detect it."

"Doctor, I'm worried for my sons," my mom said, turning toward my dad. "What if this happens to them?"

"Mrs. Pellegrino, I assure you your boys are young and healthy. They have decades before they would be in any kind of danger. Of course, that is, *if* they were born with this condition. Please keep in mind there is a good chance they were not."

"Yeah, Mom, let's not get ahead of ourselves," my brother said.

"You're right. You're right," my mom replied.

"I'll be back to check on him tonight," said Dr. Peterson.

"Thank you, Doctor," I said.

With that, he gave us a nod and left us. We retreated to each of our claimed positions around the room. I walked over to our private window. The view from this angle was a far cry from the view of the city skyline outside of the hallway window. I looked down to the streets below. They were dirty and drenched in road salt. The few people walking around were bundled up. A storm was on its way, and the temperature was dropping fast. The city was preparing for significant snowfall. Looking out the window was a way for me to escape from the pain I was going through, even for a moment.

It wasn't long before my dad had his first visitor, yet it wasn't a familiar face. A short older Black man with a protruding belly stood in the doorway. He certainly was sharply dressed. Dressed in his Sunday's best, he wore a full-length black coat and black blazer and vest with a white shirt and black silk tie. A white scarf was draped around his neck, and he wore a black fedora with white ribbon trim. We were all waist deep in our own sorrow, so no one noticed him standing there at first. My mom was the first to look up.

"Oh, hello," she said as she got up to greet him.

He took off his hat and held it against his chest. His hair was short and gray.

"Ma'am," he replied with a smile.

His teeth were crooked and yellow. Some were missing, but his smile was charming nonetheless.

"My name is Leroy Devo," he said in a raspy Louisiana accent. "But you can call me…the Buddha Man!" he said with a grin.

Now, during this time, I was introduced to so many people it would be impossible to remember all of their names; but the *Buddha Man?* That's a name you remember.

"The Buddha Man?" my mom questioned.

The man chuckled and grabbed his stomach. "Yes, ma'am! You see this belly? 'Cuz, if you rub this belly, it gives good luck! Heh-heh! You can call me Buddha for short."

That made my mom chuckle. It was the first time I had seen my mom smile in days.

"Well, Buddha, I'm Richard's wife, Diane."

"It's a pleasure," he replied as they shook hands.

"These are my sons. My oldest, Brian, and my youngest, Kevin."

We both stepped forward and shook his hand as well.

"Hey there, boys." He looked past us, at my dad. "May I?" he asked as he placed his hat back on his head.

"Of course," my mom said.

He stepped forward to my dad's bedside. He placed his hands on the bedside railing and stood quietly for a moment before speaking.

"Ayy, Richayyy! It's the Buddha Man! Good to see you, my brother. You have a beautiful family here. You better get well soon, 'ight?" He turned back to my mom. "How's he doin'?"

"Uh, not great. We just need to take this one day at a time. How exactly do you know my husband?"

"Why, we started together at Triboro over thirty years ago. We were in the same training class back in the '70s."

"Oh, so you know Billy and Frankie and all those guys?"

"Yes, ma'am. I started driving a bus when I moved to New York from New Orleans after my wife, Ellie, passed."

"Oh, I'm sorry to hear that," my mom said.

"Yeah, well…back then, I was just called the Man," he said, slapping his gut. "Buddha came a few years later."

That gave us all a laugh.

He stared at my dad once again. "Yeah, Richie's good people."

"I'm surprised this is the first time I'm hearing of you," my mom said.

I was thinking the exact same thing. What a character this guy was.

"Oh, I retired long ago. I was the oldest brother in that class. Years of driving those rigs around do a nightmare on your back. I've been working with the union most recently, trying to keep busy in my old age." His tone suddenly became more somber. "Now, Mrs. Pellegrino—"

"Please, Diane," my mom interrupted.

"Diane, Richie's in a bad way. I want to make sure you all are set up should the worst happen. You have all his paperwork regarding his pension, 401(k) benefits, etc., correct?"

My mom got nervous. She hadn't the slightest idea where my dad kept records of all that.

"Oh, uh, I'm not sure."

"No need to worry," the Buddha Man said reassuringly. "I'll go to the office and get all the documentation for you. In fact, I'll head there right now."

"Oh, thank you so much."

"You're very welcome. I'll be back in a few days to see how he's doing. I'm sure I'll be able to catch you here."

"Yes, I don't think we'll be anywhere else," my mom said lightheartedly.

"All right then." He tipped his cap. "Ma'am. Boys," he said as he made his way to the door.

"It was very nice to meet you," my mom said.

"Likewise," he replied, heading down the hallway.

"What an interesting man," said my mom.

"You never heard of him? Ever?" Kevin asked.

"No. Never."

"Wow."

The day dragged on. A nurse would come in every hour or so check on him, change out his IV, change his sheets, and anything else he needed. She was a short Asian American woman with her hair tied back in a ponytail. She was very nice and respectful toward us. She always greeted us with a smile. At least, I assume she did. She never took off her mask.

It wasn't long before my mother's cell phone rang once again. It was one of my dad's closest friends, James. James worked with my dad for the last fifteen years. Over that time, they became the best of friends. My dad recently helped him and his family buy a house in our neighborhood.

"Hi, James," my mom answered.

"Diane, I'm so sorry," said James.

"I appreciate that."

"I just can't believe Richie's gone."

"Wait. What?"

"I heard what happened over the radio. I can't get over the fact that he's dead."

"James, what are you talking about? Richard didn't die!"

"What? But he had a heart attack!"

"Yes…I mean, it's bad, but he's not dead! He's at Mercy Hospital in the ICU!"

"What! Oh my God!"

"Who told you he died?"

"They announced it over the radio to all the drivers! They said, 'Pellegrino's dead. Pellegrino's dead.' Are you telling me he's still alive?"

"Of course! I'm sitting right next to him!"

"Oh, thank God! I'm going to punch whoever made that announcement! Listen, I'm going to come down there as soon as I can."

"Absolutely. I'm sure he would appreciate it. See you soon."

"Bye, Diane."

"Bye."

My mom hung up her phone and turned to us.

"You won't believe this," she said.

"What?" Kevin asked.

"That was James. All the drivers think your father is dead! They announced it over the radio!"

"What kind of idiot would send out that kind of a message?" I said.

"I do not know," said my mom.

That would explain the limited number of visitors we had throughout the day. It pained me to think that the majority of my dad's coworkers thought he was dead. It brought me back to the morning before where I, too, believed briefly that he had died. It seemed everyone was writing him off, from the doctors to his coworkers and everyone in between. I was not about to give up on him, not about to give up hope, no matter how difficult it became.

CHAPTER 5

A BLISTERING STORM WAS SET to roll in during the night. We made it home just in time to take Eddie out. For him, it was another lonely day waiting by the window for his family to come home. We made the decision to have a family friend, Carol, take him in during this difficult time. We were not equipped to properly care for him at the moment. It was best for him. She was the one who always watched him when we went away on vacation. Eddie loved playing with her black Lab, Jack. Carol always dressed him up with a little red bandanna. Jack was a little bit older and wasn't as spry as Eddie, but they always had a good time together. He and Eddie were like best friends. Eddie hopped in Carol's car without a second thought, and they drove off.

The storm dropped nearly a foot of snow overnight. We were afraid it was going to keep us from driving out to Queens that day. The roads were bad. It was too dangerous without all-wheel drive. Lucky for us, Billy called in the morning and offered to drive us there in his Jeep. What a stroke of luck. It was extremely nice of him to come all the way out here for us. He was a true friend, and we were all extremely grateful. We waited for him inside our cold and quiet home. I stared at the aftermath of the blizzard through the front window. Heavy winds had created large snowbanks all around us. Our cars were completely buried, and the road was still unplowed. Suddenly I spotted a red Jeep pushing its way down the road.

In our heavy snow gear and boots, we trudged our way down to the street and got in Billy's truck. My mom grabbed the front seat, and my brother and I hopped in the back.

"Hey, Billy, thanks for helping us out," my mom said as she climbed in.

"Hey, guys," he said. "No problem. It was time I visited him again. Plus I wanted to make sure you guys got there okay."

"Appreciate it," I said.

"Sorry we got snow all over the floor," my brother said, looking down at the icy mess we brought into the truck with us.

"Don't worry about it. This thing has seen worse."

Local roads were a mess, but the expressway was fairly clear. An army of plow trucks cleared the road in time for the morning commute. It was the least congested I had seen so far. Smart people took the day off. It was an excellent time to sleep in, enjoy a cup of hot cocoa, and spend some quality time with the family. We, on the other hand, didn't have that luxury.

It took some time, but we got there. For the first time, we were able to get a spot on the street close to the hospital. Billy powered his Jeep up and over a snowbank. I climbed out and helped my mom out so she wouldn't slip. The sidewalks were icy and slippery. Not a lot of it was clear, so it forced us at times to walk in the street. We walked through the hospital main entrance. Billy wasn't family, so he needed a visitors' pass to make it up to the ICU. As we got off the elevator and walked down the hall, the nurses greeted us. We were becoming familiar to them, like regulars at the neighborhood bar.

There was my dad, right where we left him. We greeted him as we usually did. My mom announced our presence as we walked into the room. She walked over and kissed his forehead.

"Hi, hun. Billy drove us today. We got hit with a foot of snow last night," she said as she stroked his hair. "But don't worry. We made it."

"Hey, Rich," Billy said.

I looked down at my dad in his bed. Something was different. It puzzled me because I couldn't quite put my finger on it. I stared at him until I suddenly figured it out. The bulky ice packs that lined his body under the sheets were missing. As soon as a nurse walked in while making his rounds, I questioned him about it.

"Hi, excuse me," I said.

"What's up, brother?" he said as he greeted me with a smile.

"There were ice packs around him. Do you know if and why they were removed?"

"Yep. He doesn't need them anymore, so we removed them early this morning."

"What do you mean by 'He doesn't need them anymore'?" my mom asked.

"See, the reason for the ice packs was to keep his internal body temperature low to slow down the negative reactions within him and prevent as much damage as possible. We can't leave the ice packs on very long because eventually his body temperature has to go back up to normal."

"So the ice packs did their job?" I asked.

"They did all they could do. It's up to him now."

"Man. Okay, thanks."

"You got it, man. Anything you guys need, just let me know."

"We appreciate it," said my mom. "What's your name by the way?"

"Colt. Colt Jameson," he replied.

That was probably the most badass name I have ever heard. It fit him well. His arms were ripped, with one fully tattooed down to his knuckles. He had long pushed-back hair and a trimmed beard. That, coupled with his young face and inviting smile, made him appear to be the perfect combination of tough and friendly.

"Great name," I said.

Nurse Colt smiled and said, "Appreciate it, brother. I'll be back in a few to check on you guys."

A short while after that, I found myself pacing around. It drove my mom and brother crazy. They told me to either sit still or go walk out into the hall. I couldn't sit still. I was extremely anxious and antsy. I walked into the hall where the scene outside that old, familiar window caught my eye. The sun was peering through the winter clouds. Its rays bounced off the snow-covered rooftops and reflected off the Manhattan high-rises across the river. It was so calm and peaceful. I closed my eyes and took a deep breath. At that moment, I felt a small wave of relief wash over me.

I looked over once again at the elderly woman in 12B. She lay still in her bed, but she seemed awake and alert. There were less visitors today although they seemed to be in good spirits. I could hear her heart-rate monitor from the hallway. Its beep was slow and steady. I was relieved to see her doing better. If this elderly woman, as frail and lifeless as she seemed, could hang in there, then maybe my dad could do the same. I headed back into my dad's room and looked at him lying there. With that breathing tube down his throat and all those machines around, I fought to keep that level of optimism.

As we sat in our routine silence, my dad started to receive a steady flow of visitors. First of which was James. My dad's closest friend came in as soon as his shift ended. He stood in the doorway for a moment before he entered. I almost didn't recognize him. He was normally clean shaven but was now sporting a full beard. It was coarse and gray. He later explained it was his new winter look. His winter look must have included gaining some weight because it looked like he packed on a few pounds recently.

"James, you made it," my mom said as we all got up to greet him.

I noticed his eyes were red and watery. His face was flush.

"Of course," he replied. He looked over at my dad. "You know, this made me realize something. I really only have two friends in this world, my brother...and Richie."

His voice cracked at the last second as he held back tears. This, of course, brought my mom to tears. She gave him a hug. He walked over; took off his cap, revealing his shaved head; and just stared down at my dad for a moment.

"How's he doing?" James said.

From behind, my mom took a breath and replied.

"Uh...well, he's not getting any worse, but we're not sure what's going to happen to him."

"Did they say if he'll wake up?" he asked.

"They are not sure honestly."

There wasn't much else to say. There wasn't any good news. It was as if we were all sitting at the edge of our seats for the past few days waiting for something, anything, to go in our favor. James sat with us for some time. The occasional chitchat between Billy, my mom, and him helped make time go by faster, anything to divert my attention away from the haunting beeps of the heart-rate monitors. James was a great storyteller with an exceptional memory. He would regal us with stories from the job, the company softball games, and alike. For a moment, our spirits were lifted.

"I hope I'm not interrupting," called a familiar voice.

We all turned our heads toward the door. The Buddha Man was back! He appeared as sharply dressed as ever with the same yellow-toothed grin as before. This time, he was sporting a white fedora with black trim.

"Jimmy?" he exclaimed.

"Buddha!" James cried out.

They hadn't seen each other since Buddha retired. It was a sweet reunion. They embraced each other with a big bear hug. He gave my mom a hug hello as well and shook both my and my brother's hands. He held a manila folder under his right arm.

"Ah! Are those the documents you said were so graciously going to look up for me?" my mom asked when she noticed the folder.

The Buddha Man grabbed the folder from under his arm and held it for a moment.

"Uh, yes. Yes, they are."

A distinct change in his voice could be detected. It changed to a tone I had heard a lot recently.

"Why don't we step into the hall for a moment? There's some things we need to discuss."

"Um, okay, sure," my mom cautiously replied.

They both stepped outside and gathered by the hallway window I had become so familiar with. I could tell something was up, so I quietly stood at the edge of the doorway to listen in. They were just barely within earshot.

"As I said, I went down to the records office and pulled all documentation regarding Richie's retirement benefits."

"Okay," my mom said, bracing herself for what she could only assume was bad news coming her way.

"Well, now everything was seemingly in order," he said, opening the folder. "It says right here, in the event of his passing, all of Richie's retirement accounts—401(k), pension, insurances—will go to the beneficiary below."

"Okay, so what's the problem?"

He turned the folder and handed it to her. He pointed to a specific section.

"Read on," he replied.

My mom glanced at the paperwork Buddha presented to her. For a moment, she didn't grasp what he was trying to demonstrate. Then it hit her. Her jaw dropped like a stone in a shallow river. The color washed away from her face. She looked up at the Buddha Man, then back down at the piece of paper.

"This can't be right! There has to be a mistake."

"No mistake. I wish it was. That is the most up-to-date file we had. Believe me, I checked and checked."

"I can't believe this."

The writing on the form was clear as day. Where it said "name of spouse" under the beneficiary section, it did not say my mom's name. Instead it read:

Sofia Pellegrino

"I don't understand. How is his ex-wife's name still on here? They divorced over thirty years ago!"

Ex-wife? I thought to myself. *My dad was married before he met my mother? Why was this the first time I was hearing about this? How could they keep such a secret from their children? What else don't we know?*

This was a complete shock to me. My head filled with such uncertainty.

"I'm guessin', after he got remarried, Rich forgot to change the name on the beneficiary form, and after so many years, it got lost in the shuffle."

"Well, what happens if he passes?" my mom questioned as her anger started to rise.

"Unfortunately all benefits from your husband's entire tenure with the company would go to this, uh, Sofia woman."

"To hell with that!" My mom raised her voice, which started to grab the attention of the hospital staff and other visitors.

"Mrs. Pellegrino, please, lower your voice!" Buddha said, trying to regain control over the situation.

"I'm his wife! Besides, she died years ago! Richard even forgot her name!"

"I realize that, ma'am, but according to his employer, this woman is his wife, dead or not."

"So nobody gets anything?" my mom asked furiously. She pleaded with him, "Buddha...Leroy, there has to be a way to fix this."

He stepped closer and spoke quietly, "Look, the only person who can alter the name on this form is Rich."

My mom cut him off, "But he's unconscious."

"Yes! That's why I brought this," the Buddha Man said as he carefully pulled a sheet of paper out from his manila folder. "See now, I'm not supposed to tell you this, but with his signature on this piece of paper, you would be named the new beneficiary."

"And how exactly are we supposed to get him to sign it?"

He took a pen out of his jacket pocket. "You take this pen and, with me or one of your sons or whoever as a witness, put it in his hand, and move it so he signs right here on the line. It can be just a scribble. I'll verify it."

"I can't do that!" my mom nervously whispered back at him.

"Sure you can! Just make sure no one else sees."

"Oh, I don't know," she said, now holding the pen and paper.

"I'm sorry, but that's our only option. I wish there was more I could do."

"Oh, no," my mom said, putting her hand on his shoulder. "You've done plenty. I'll think about it. Thank you."

At the conclusion of their meeting, they proceeded back into my dad's room. It was there I waited.

As they turned the corner, I stood on the other side of the wall. I pounced at first sight of my mom.

"Dad was married?"

My mom was startled. "What? Were you listening?" was all she could respond with.

"Never mind that. How come you never told us?"

"Brian, it was so long ago. I guess it never crossed our minds."

That was not the answer I was looking for. "Never crossed your minds?"

"Brian, not now. I have a lot on my mind."

"Don't we all?" I replied.

"That's enough!" my mom scolded me.

"What's going on?" Kevin said.

He, Billy, and James were having a conversation about who knows what on the other side of the room; but the arguing between my mom and me grabbed their attention.

"Did you know Dad had a wife before Mom?" I asked.

"He did?" Kevin replied.

"Yes!"

"Oh, so?"

"So?"

I was shocked at his lackluster response. He was generally the more hotheaded one out of the two of us. He had been known to fly off the handle at a moment's notice while I, on the other hand, was the complete opposite—always cool, calm, and collected. In a shocking reversal, I was the one flipping out while Kevin didn't seem fazed.

"That doesn't bother you?" I asked as I felt myself come back down to earth.

"Well…it's surprising, but I think we have bigger things to worry about," he replied, gesturing toward our unconscious father.

Boy, did that put me in my place. While I was disappointed that this information was kept from us, it paled in comparison to the possibility of losing a parent. I felt horrible for yelling at my mom. I knew what she was going through, especially now with this new financial burden looming over all of our heads. I looked toward her, getting teary eyed.

"Sorry," I mouthed at her.

She gave a big hug as all was forgiven.

With a sniffle, I gathered myself and said, "I'm going to grab something to eat."

"I'm hungry too. I'll go with you," said Kevin.

I would have rather been alone, but my brother didn't take the hint. We both walked down to the cafeteria to have some of that barely edible food we all loved so much. My mom tucked the folder in her purse. She sat down; rather, she dropped into the chair beside my dad's bed. She threw her head back against the wall.

"You really never told the boys about Richie's first wife?" Billy asked as he walked over to her.

"No. I don't know why honestly. I guess, after a while, her existence faded out of both of our minds."

"I never had the pleasure of meeting this woman," James said.

"You didn't miss much," said Billy, being the only one who knew my dad during that time in his life. "She wasn't the most pleasant person, but Richie was young and stupid."

"I've been there," said James, being married multiple times as well.

My brother and I rejoined them around twenty minutes later. I brought my mom a sandwich from the cafeteria wrapped in cellophane. I offered it to her, to which she thanked me but didn't eat. I hadn't seen her eat in days. It began to worry me.

Eventually James and the Buddha Man said their goodbyes and headed home. They both had lives to live and families to take care of. No one expected to stay all day like we did. To stop by, even for a moment, was always appreciated. It was nice to see people thinking of us in our time of need. This was only the beginning. We could never have prepared for the outpouring of affection that we were soon to receive.

CHAPTER 6

THE NEXT FEW DAYS BLENDED together. The temperature rose, and the roads cleared. My brother gave me a break from driving one day, but I drove the rest of the time. The trek to and from the hospital, whether during the day or night, became easier and easier—almost routine, as sad of a notion as that is. They were quiet car rides with nothing but the roar of the engine to keep me entertained. We didn't listen to music. We didn't talk amongst ourselves either. Everyone just stared off at the horizon. The only time my mom ever said anything was to ask me to turn up the heat.

I could have never foreseen the number of visitors my dad had received over the last few days. It was like an endless parade of bus drivers and other workers making their way through our little corner of the hospital. People of all walks of life—different colors and creeds, old, young, male, and female—were all coming to show their support and to wish us and my dad well. Some people, I knew or met in passing. Most of them, however, I had never seen or heard of. It got pretty crowded at times. They certainly were a lively and spirited group. They would tell stories and laugh or occasionally cry well into the evening. The nursing staff often had to step in and ask us to keep it down to a dull roar. Apparently the lobby of the hospital was only supposed to let a limited number of visitors up at a time, but someone clearly wasn't doing their job.

Each person who snuck their way past the front desk seemed to have a heartwarming story or anecdote regarding my dad. One in particular was told by a man by the name of Eric Ibanez. Eric was a younger guy, only on the payroll for a few years. He grew up in a struggling mostly Hispanic community not too far from the bus depot. He started driving a bus when he was just twenty-two, extremely young by public transportation standards. One day, a few months after Eric started, my dad caught him sleeping on his bus after it was supposed to have pulled out a half an hour prior. Eric apologized and apologized, claiming that he was exhausted because he had to get a second job to help his mom pay the rent. He explained that his father had passed away unexpectedly and his mom couldn't do it on her own.

My dad was sympathetic. There was a zero-tolerance policy when it came to sleeping in buses whether in the depot or on the road. If it had been any other supervisor who had caught Eric asleep on the job, they would have fired him on the spot, but not my dad. He would rather him not fall asleep behind the wheel. My dad agreed to just keep it between them. Eric was so grateful that he never slept on a bus or clocked in late ever again. In fact, my dad kind of looked after him from that point on. He tried to give him the easiest route whenever possible. He would buy his lunch on occasion, and he was always on the lookout for overtime opportunities for Eric. I think my dad saw a lot of his sons when he looked at Eric. He wasn't too much older than us. That is probably what made him look out for the rookie driver.

My dad was also a financial wiz. Some might say a penny-pincher, but he knew how to save money. This was no news to me. For example, when my brother and I were young and he would take us out for kids' meals, we would always ask for cheeseburgers. However, he would order my brother and me hamburgers. Whenever I would say, "But, Daddy, I wanted a cheeseburger!" he would reply with "We have cheese at home." So to save a quarter, we would take a slice out of our fridge at home and put it on our burgers. Voila! A cheeseburger.

I never realized that he was passing his financial knowledge onto others as well. Many of my dad's coworkers had financial troubles. It was just a fact of the times. Driving a bus wasn't going to make anyone rich, but it was honest work. Derrick Jones, another driver, had worked with my dad for years. He had a lovely wife named Liz and two young daughters. They didn't have much, but they had each other. Unfortunately, one day, Liz was diagnosed with stage-4 breast cancer. The chances of survival were slim at best. It was extremely hard, but they fought this disease together. They poured their life savings into experimental treatments and methods.

They fought tooth and nail through all the trials and hardships. Unfortunately, only six months after her initial diagnosis, Liz passed away, leaving Derrick to parent his two young daughters by himself. With his life savings all but gone and only one source of income, he struggled to provide for his family. He confided in my dad when he went back to work after laying his wife to rest. My dad was determined to help Derrick get back on his feet. He pushed him into signing up for a 401(k). My dad was a big fan of them, especially since the company matched their contributions. He called it "free money." My dad also worked as Derrick's personal accountant. He looked for ways to save wherever he could, from groceries to car insurance.

One final thing my dad pushed him to do, which Derrick wouldn't even consider at first, was moving into a cheaper apartment. Derrick's rent was extremely high, much too high for a single-income family. He refused to move, claiming that there were too many memories of his wife in that apartment and he didn't want to leave them behind.

"Do it for your girls," my dad would say. "You will take the memories with you. At this rate, you'll be forced out of your apartment soon enough. Would you rather have your daughters live on the street?"

It was harsh but effective. Derrick got the point and found a cheaper apartment for him and his family. He saved every penny he could using the methods my dad gave him and invested in his future by opening a 401(k). He couldn't stress enough when he spoke with us how grateful he was for my dad's financial advice. It saved his family.

As I said earlier, not all the drivers were men. There were a handful of female drivers in the mix. My dad was visited one day by a woman named Ronda Jefferson. She was a tall, heavyset middle-aged Black woman with short, curly black hair. She wore designer glasses and an assortment of silver jewelry and had long multicolored acrylic nails.

She walked in slow and steady, leaning to the side of her oversized handbag weighing her down. Her face dropped at the sight of my comatose father.

"Poor Richie" were the first words out of her mouth.

She sat with us for a while. I gave her my chair as she claimed she had a bad knee and couldn't stand for very long. She couldn't express the amount of respect she had for my dad. She explained being a woman in a predominantly male workplace was a challenge. She always felt that she didn't receive the same amount of respect as her male counterparts. My dad always treated her with the respect she deserved. He greeted her every morning with a smile and didn't favor any driver over another. Ronda always appreciated that. She said it made her job so much easier.

I grew increasingly prouder of my dad after hearing all these stories about him. It wasn't just how he was so open to helping others. It was the fact that he never boasted about it. He never bragged or sought praise for any of his good deeds. To him, he was just doing his job.

CHAPTER 7

A week had passed since my dad's heart gave out on him. Each day blended into the next. It was the longest week of my life, and yet it felt like everything was happening at once. Word had spread throughout the neighborhood. Our refrigerator was full of food from neighbors and my mom's coworkers as a way to show their support. One couple brought an entire deli platter. A neighbor dropped off an entire fried chicken dinner with all the trimmings. One morning, the old couple from across the street brought us donuts and bagels. It was greatly appreciated, but I couldn't bring myself to chitchat about my unconscious father with my elderly neighbors. So I hid in my room as they spoke with my mom in the kitchen. I emerged when they finally left. They left an impressive spread behind with a dozen bagels, cream cheese, butter, and a half-dozen donuts. I grabbed a glazed donut for breakfast and got myself dressed.

Nicole joined us on the trip to the hospital today. She skipped out on class to be there for my family and me. My brother, on the other hand, stayed behind to go to his classes. We missed so much the week before. My mom didn't want us to flunk the semester, so she told us both to go to class to get as much information about finals as we could. Kevin went in first, and the following day, we would swap. I would go to class while he and Mom would drive to the hospital.

Nicole was nervous. She held my hand tight as we entered the hospital. It felt good having her there, having someone to lean on for support. The halls of the ICU were decorated in the holiday spirit. Cutouts of Christmas trees, snowflakes, menorahs, and other symbols of the season lined the walls. Mistletoe was hung over the nurses' station, and a few nurses even wore Christmas lights around their necks.

I tried to explain to Nicole what to expect when she saw my dad for the first time so she wouldn't be in too much shock. My mom entered my dad's room ahead of us. Nicole and I were right behind her when the room across the hall caught my attention. I stopped in my tracks. My hand broke free of Nicole's grasp. She turned and looked at me puzzled.

"Babe, you okay?" she asked.

The room, once filled with family and with life and love, was now empty and dark. The bed was empty. The white sheets were cleaned, pressed, and folded. I turned to grab the attention of the first nurse or doctor I could find. I spotted an older nurse walking out of a room just down the hall.

"Excuse me!" I called out to her.

"Yes?" she replied.

"The woman that was here for the past week. Did she go home?"

"Oh, no. She passed away overnight."

How could that be? She seemed to be doing so well. For some reason, the news of this woman's passing affected me deeply. She was a complete stranger to me. Why was I feeling this way? Perhaps the idea of seeing this feeble, frail old woman make a full recovery in my mind served as a sign of hope for me and my family. Now that hope was diminished. I could feel my stomach drop. My face went numb, my expression blank. I felt a tug at my arm.

"Baby," said Nicole. "Baby, what's wrong?"

Just then, I snapped back to reality. "What? Oh, nothing. I'm fine," I said when I came to.

"You sure?" she asked, her face full of concern.

"Yes," I said as I put on a brave face. I took her hand once more. "C'mon. Let's go."

We turned around and walked in the room. It was then Nicole had her first glance at my dad in the state that he was in. She placed her free hand over her mouth. Her eyes started to water.

"Oh my God."

My mom was waiting for us on the opposite side of my dad's bed.

"Everything all right?" she asked.

"Yeah, everything's fine," I replied.

"Say hello," my mom told Nicole.

She looked at her for a moment, then looked up at me. "What do I say?" she asked.

We've all been there. I recalled having a similar thought when I spoke to him on day one.

"Just say hi. I'm pretty sure he can hear us," my mom said.

Nicole stepped forward to my dad's bedside. I stood beside her and put my arm around her.

"Hi, Mr. Pellegrino." Her voice cracked slightly. "It's…it's Nicole. I'm so sorry this happened to you. I know you'll be okay."

She looked up at me as if asking for approval, to see if she said the right thing. I looked down at her and gave her a smile and a nod. It was good to have her there. Sure, my family and I were going through this together, but we all retreated into our own spaces to cope with the situation in our own ways. Nicole was removed just enough from the situation to be a shoulder for me to lean on. Her priority was to make sure I got through it all in one piece. I will always be grateful to have her at my side.

After about twenty minutes of letting my girl-friend soak it all in, Dr. Peterson stopped by, except this time he wasn't alone. Another doctor was at his side. She was slightly over five feet tall, about Nicole's height, and had short, curly hair. By looking at her, I would say she was around forty years old. She had a comforting and approachable look about her, much more so than Dr. Peterson. She wore a bright-pink turtleneck sweater under the stereotypical white coat and stethoscope.

"How's everyone doing today?" Dr. Peterson asked.

"We're okay," my mom replied. "Doctor, I'd like you to meet my son's girlfriend, Nicole."

"Nice to meet you," he said to Nicole.

"Likewise," Nicole replied.

"I would like to introduce you to my colleague Dr. Rodriguez. She's one of our top neurologists."

"Hello," she said with a smile.

"Tell them why you're here, Doctor," Dr. Peterson said to Dr. Rodriguez.

She stepped forward and addressed the family. She spoke calmly and confidently.

"So over the last week, we performed multiple CAT scans on Richard's brain. Each one came back inconclusive. Due to swelling in his brain, we couldn't see much. That is, however, until last night. Finally the swelling went down enough for us to get a clear look into the state of his brain tissue." She paused for a second and smiled. "And I am pleased to say everything looked pretty good."

"Does this mean he's going to wake up?" I asked.

"That is why we are here," Dr. Rodriguez continued. "Right now, he is in what we call a medically assisted coma. This basically means we are keeping him in a comalike state, using certain medications such as propofol, to keep the body's activity at a minimum to help both the body and the brain heal. By the looks of his last CAT scan, it would appear to have paid off."

"So what happens now?" my mom asked with a hint of optimism in her voice.

Dr. Peterson spoke up, "Well, that's why we're here. We are going to slowly wean your husband off these medications and try to get a response."

"Oh, wow! Okay!" my mom said, praying that this was the break we all had been waiting for—that her husband, my father, would come back to us.

"So shall we begin?" Dr. Rodriguez asked Dr. Peterson.

"Yes. The sooner, the better," he replied.

My mom, Nicole, and I all held hands. Tears were starting to drip down our faces. I was shivering with anticipation. Dr. Rodriguez walked over to the control unit in charge of distributing the various medications into his bloodstream. Like a captain at the helm of a ship, she began turning dials and pressing buttons. It was faint, but we could hear the whirl of the machine die down as Dr. Rodriguez reduced the flow of propofol to one hundred milligrams. We all waited a few moments for the drugs to wear off a bit. Both doctors intensely watched the monitors for any abrupt changes in his vitals. Once he was satisfied, Dr. Peterson began to run some tests. He walked over to the foot of the bed and uncovered my dad's feet. He ran the end of a pen up and down the arch of his foot to check for signs of paralysis. He then grabbed his toes and started to move them around. He turned to Dr. Rodriguez.

"I got a slight twitch when I touch right here," he said.

That was a positive sign that he still had feeling in his legs and feet.

Dr. Rodriguez responded by further reducing the amount of medication coursing through my dad's veins.

"Reducing propofol to fifty milligrams," she said as she adjusted the flow of the IV.

Dr. Peterson moved to the side of my dad's bed for another test. Everything was leaning on its very outcome. Bracing himself on the bedside railing, he gently leaned in close to my dad.

"Mr. Pellegrino," he said gently in my dad's ear. He waited a moment, but no visible response. He tried again, except louder this time. "Mr. Pellegrino!"

Still nothing. We were all on the edge of our seats holding on to each other with every fiber of our being. This was a make-or-break moment.

Dr. Peterson tried one last time. "Richie!"

That did it! The second my dad's name left the doctor's lips, his face twitched ever so slightly. Dr. Peterson nearly jumped back at my dad's reaction. He quickly stood upright and turned to the monitor behind him. My dad's pulse on the heart-rate monitor displayed a momentary spike in his heartbeat! He was still in there! We were all gleaming with hope. Tears ran down our faces. Both doctors looked at each other. They had signs of both shock and optimism on their faces.

Suddenly the monitor started to beep intensely. Its warning lights flashed red. We all turned to realize that his heart rate and blood pressure were skyrocketing. There was barely any time for the doctors to react before…flat line.

"Oh my God!" my mom cried.

All readings on the screen dropped to zero. A deafening high-pitched tone, one you only hope you hear on TV or in movies, pierced the air. Both doctors quickly sprang into action.

"Dammit!" Doctor Peterson exclaimed. He began doing chest compressions. "I need a crash cart!"

On cue, the nurses, who saw the alert on their station computers, rushed in with a crash cart armed with a defibrillator. Dr. Rodriguez rushed over to us.

"We need to get you out of here," she said, trying to push us toward the door.

My mom stood her ground. "No! I'm not leaving him!" she cried through her tears.

"Ma'am, please!" the doctor insisted.

I turned to my mom. "Mom, let's go! Let them work! He will be okay!"

Did I mean that? I wasn't even sure myself, but it worked. The three of us rushed into the hallway. My mom's legs no longer had the strength to hold her up. She grabbed my arm tight to support her weight. Nurse Colt ran over and helped her stay on her feet. We walked her over to a chair, where she sat bawling into the palms of her hands.

Inside the nurses were getting the defibrillator into position. Dr. Peterson ripped open my dad's hospital gown. He placed the paddles on my dad's chest.

"Clear!" he announced.

My dad's body jerked, but still no heartbeat. Once the defibrillator reached full power, he did it again.

"Clear!"

The high-pitched tone rang on. The doctor tried one more time.

"Clear!"

It got quiet. One beat…two beats. He was back. Everyone could breathe a sigh of relief.

We waited down the hall. Nicole sat beside my mom with her arms around her. I stood, staring down the hall. The warning light above the room's doorway, which had been glowing red, had turned off. Moments later, Dr. Peterson emerged. His face was red and sweaty. He took a handkerchief out from his back pocket and wiped his brow. He then slowly approached.

"Is he…," I said.

"He's stable once again," the doctor replied.

"What happened this time?" my mom asked with quivering lips.

The doctor hesitated. He didn't really have an answer for us. As much as we would like them to have all the answers, sometimes you just have to accept the fact that doctors can only do so much. They are not gods. They cannot command life or death at their will.

"I wish I had an answer that would put you at some kind of ease, but I don't. We've done all we could for Richard. It's up to him now. The best we can do is make sure he's comfortable."

Part of me wanted to say "That's not good enough! Get back in there," but I knew he was trying his best.

"Thank you, Doctor," I said, shaking his hand.

Dr. Peterson nodded his head, his face filled with defeat and exhaustion. He turned slowly and shuffled away. Both my mom and Nicole sat there crying. I watched him move down the hall, take a breath, and grab the next chart, on to the next patient barely clinging to life.

After a moment to compose ourselves, we reentered my dad's room. All of his vitals were calm for the moment. I stood over him. After looking down for a moment, I spoke up.

"Mom, you still have that paperwork right? That the Buddha Man gave you?"

She didn't answer me. She just grabbed her purse. After sifting through it, she pulled out the folder the Buddha Man handed her a few days prior. She stared at it for a moment. Her eyes pointed in my direction as she held it up for me to see.

"I don't understand," said Nicole. "What paperwork are you talking about?"

"Remember the issue with my dad's benefits I told you about? Well, if we can get his signature on one of those forms right there, it would solve everything!"

"Brian, that's fraud. He needs to be conscious to sign, and there is no way that's happening now. You saw what just happened!" said my mom.

"That's my point! Who knows if they can bring him back if this happens again. We're running out of time!"

"But he's unconscious, like your mom said. How are we supposed to get his signature?" Nicole asked.

"We put a pen in his hand like Buddha said. We ask someone, a nurse or a doctor, to, I don't know, say he came to just long enough to give us his signature. Then we just move his hand and make a mark on the dotted line."

"Brian, who's going to risk doing that?" asked my mom.

Right at that moment, Nurse Colt poked his head in. "Excuse me."

"Oh, Nurse Colt," said my mom. "Sorry, we were just having a little family discussion."

"Yes, I know. I'm sorry, but I overheard your family's problem."

"Oh, you did?" I asked.

"Yeah, and well, I just wanted to offer up my assistance."

"Oh, you don't have to do that," said my mom.

I stared daggers at her. I didn't want her to ruin possibly our only shot at this.

"No, I know that. Your family's been through hell lately. I can tell. If I can help make sure you guys are covered, I'm happy to do so. I'll be your witness, if that's what you need."

"Won't you get into trouble?" Nicole asked.

"Psh, nah," he replied with a wave of his hand. "I would expect someone to do the same for me if I were in your shoes."

"Why, thank you!" said my mom, getting emotional once again. "This means so much."

"You're welcome," the nurse replied. He came in close and got really quiet. "Here's what we'll do. I'll come back in a few minutes while making my rounds to check on him. Have the form and a pen ready. I'll close the curtain to give us some privacy, and you do what you need to do."

He then looked over at Nicole and me. "Perhaps it might be best for you two to step out during this time. One witness is enough, and we don't need added attention."

"It sounds like you've done this before," I added jokingly.

He kind of smirked and said, "You can't always play by the book."

About thirty minutes later, Nurse Colt was making his rounds. He was one room away, and we were ready. My mom found a pen and had the form on her lap. I could hear him walking toward us.

"Okay, this should only take a second," said Nurse Colt as he entered the room with his clipboard under his arm.

He winked at me. That was our cue to get out of there.

"Want to grab something from the vending machine?" I asked Nicole.

"Sure," she replied.

As we headed out, Colt pulled the privacy curtain around my dad's bed. He pulled the clipboard from under his arm and gave it to my mom.

"Here. Use this to write on."

My mom placed the form on top of the clipboard. She grabbed my dad's limp left hand and wrapped his fingers around the end of the pen. As she held his fingers tight around the pen with one hand, she used the other to guide the tip of the pen into position. Colt held the clipboard steady.

"Take your time," he said.

My mom took a deep breath, then slowly lowered the pen. When the pen finally hit the paper, my mom maneuvered my dad's hand to form a capital R. Then she scribbled a P and drew a couple of loops. Essentially that was what my dad's signature typically looked like. It wasn't pretty, but it was done. My mom could breathe a huge sigh of relief. The nurse pulled back the curtain.

"Okay! We're done!" Colt voiced as if he just finished a minor procedure.

"Thank you so much," my mom whispered.

Nurse Colt just winked and headed for the door. He passed by me and Nicole in the hall, holding a couple of sodas. He gave me a fist bump. It all went according to plan. We walked back in, and my mom held up the signed piece of paper. Thank God, one less thing to worry about. Now, if the worst should happen, we had the coverage we needed. I just hoped it would never come to that.

CHAPTER 8

WE STUCK TO OUR PLAN for the next day. Kevin and my mom drove to the hospital, and I stayed behind. He cursed us for making him stay home after learning what transpired the day before. He was just looking for someone to blame, someone to yell at. No one forced him to go to class that morning. He agreed it was necessary. I, on the other hand, needed a day to recuperate. The mental and physical toll this ordeal had inflicted on my body seemed insurmountable.

My mom and brother left the house early as usual. I didn't have to go to class for another couple of hours, so I lay in bed fully awake. I listened to them walk out the door, get into the car, and drive off. All the while, I lay there, staring up at the ceiling. I didn't want to leave my bed. I didn't want to move. Unbearable thoughts of me coming to terms with my dad's eventual demise had kept me up all night. Now I just lay still, my mind a blank slate. I was exhausted yet couldn't sleep.

Finally I mustered enough strength to drag myself out of bed. I headed to the bathroom and looked at myself in the mirror. There were bags under my eyes. My eyes were red and puffy. My skin was pale and dried out by the cold December air. My face even appeared thinner. I'm sure I lost a pound or two. I wasn't eating much. Like a zombie moving mindlessly about, I found myself in the kitchen. I opened the refrigerator door and rummaged through days of leftovers and untouched food. I grabbed a day-old donut and shoved it in my mouth.

I stood in the living room, chocolate frosting smeared on my lips, staring at our once-vibrant and healthy tree. It still stood, with not one spec of Christmas decoration on its wilting branches. That's what we get for getting a live tree. We always get it too early. By Christmas morning, there're always ten times more pine needles on the floor under the tree than there are gifts. Still I kept watering it. I tried my best to keep it alive for as long as I could. With no lights or decorations up throughout the house, you couldn't even tell it was almost Christmas; and with no rambunctious canine running around, the house was quiet and dull. All I could hear was the occasional hiss of the boiler and the clanging of the ice machine.

I managed to get dressed and go to class. It was about a fifteen-minute drive from my house to the college, winding through side streets and waiting at railroad crossings. My car's suspension squeaked when I drove over the tracks. The parking lot, as expansive as it was, was full. I managed to find a spot all the way in the back. I trudged through slush and road salt to get to the building in which my first class was held. Luckily all but two of my courses posted their final dates and review materials online. My goal today was to walk into these two classes, get all the information I needed, and get the hell out.

First up, Physics 101. I wasn't concerned. I had been doing very well all semester. What could I have possibly missed in one week? I walked into the lecture hall and stopped when I noticed the whiteboard. It was one of those extra-tall boards, the kind you need a ladder to write anything toward the top. The entire thing was filled with equations and formulas. From top to bottom and from left to right, there wasn't an inch of free space. I just stared at it for a moment with my jaw on the floor. I suddenly felt less confident. I composed myself and found my seat. As the class went on, my confidence grew. Of course, the stuffy old professor took his sweet time going over the material. He waited until the very end of the class to give the date and time of the final: December 23 at 8:15 a.m. At this school, they go right up until Christmas Eve.

One more to go, statistics. I had some time to kill until the class started, so I grabbed some lunch. I don't know what was worse, the food from the hospital cafeteria or the campus cafeteria. Perhaps they had the same supplier. After an hour, I headed over to my statistics class. I always found mathematics to be extremely easy, so I didn't need to sit through any review. I just needed to know when to show up for the final exam.

I had to walk all the way across campus in the freezing cold to reach it. Once everyone found their seats, the class began. The professor was a jovial older man who kept a relaxed atmosphere and liked to tell stories throughout his lessons. He always had a smile on his face and liked to engage with his students. With that, he pulled his chair out from behind his desk and placed it in front. He sat down with his legs crossed as he took questions. This was problematic for me because I now had to squeeze by him on my way to the door. He rambled on and on. All I wanted to know was the date and time. I was getting anxious and frustrated. I couldn't focus. I started to think about my dad. Finally he spit it out. It was scheduled right after the physics final. No problem. I got all the information I needed, so I prepared to leave in a hurry. I grabbed my books and proceeded toward the door. The professor was in midsentence when I crossed in front of him. With just a few more strides until freedom, he stopped me.

"Um, excuse me, sir," he said with a smile.

I stopped in my tracks, turned, and faced him.

"Where are you going?" he asked but not in a meddling way.

He was genuinely concerned I would miss important information. I opened my mouth, but I felt myself getting emotional. My voice cracked, and I started to stutter.

"I...uh...I" was all I could get out.

The professor could see the emotion on my face and the pain in my voice and said, "Okay. Go, go," as he sent me off with a wave of his hand.

I turned, and I sped out of there. With my head down, I power walked all the way to the car. My feet were wet and cold. I was shivering. When I finally got in the car and shut the door behind me is when the floodgates opened. Something came over me. I began to bawl like a baby. I rested my forehead on the steering wheel as tears streamed down my face. I pounded on the seat. All the fear and all the anger—everything was coming out at once. I missed my dad. I missed my dog. I missed how things used to be. I felt alone. I just wanted life to get back to normal. After I somewhat regained my composure, I started the car and drove home.

CHAPTER 9

ANOTHER WEEK PASSED. MY DAD had now been comatose for fourteen days. Still we came every day to sit by his side. Some days, we stayed longer than others. Some days, we stayed for the morning while, other days, we came at night. This was our life now. No longer did it seem strange or unfamiliar. I came to know the area very well. I knew the best places to park, where to find the best street vendor for a hot dog or a pretzel, and which ones to avoid. We also got to know every nurse's name by heart, on both shifts. There was Nancy, the old, seasoned veteran who didn't play games. She could be coarse and even brutally honest at times but had a heart of gold. There was Michelle, the heavyset Jamaican woman who wouldn't take any BS from anyone. Of course, there was Nurse Colt, the only male nurse on the floor. Of course, that didn't keep him from having pride in his job. There were so many other great, talented people working in that ICU it is impossible to name them all, but each one was valued highly in their own right.

We brought in some Christmas decorations to liven up the place. My mom brought a small artificial fluorescent tree from home. She placed it on the windowsill over the radiator. At night, we turned the lights down low and just stared at it. Its fiber-optic lights glistened as waves of color washed over the faux pine needles. We also brought in a Santa Claus hat one day, which we placed on my dad's head. Anything to put a smile on our faces even if it was just for a moment.

Visitation certainly died down. At one time, people were spilling out into the hallway. Now we might see one or two people per day. To be fair, a lot of my dad's coworkers came during the night, after we had already gone. At least that is, according to the nurses. One person we all were surprised to not have seen was Jerry Russo, the man who arguably was the reason my dad had lasted this long. It was possible our paths just never crossed.

One day, we stayed later than usual. The sun set hours ago. Most visitors had left the building; and the patients, those who were conscious, had fallen asleep. We dimmed all the lights in my dad's room. The only source of light came from the hallway. We were all on our phones. The white light of the touch screens shined in our faces. It strained my eyes. I had to look away. I looked up from my phone for just a moment to see a dark figure standing in the doorway with the glow of the hallway lights surrounding him. At well over six feet tall and at least three hundred pounds, he was a mountain of a man. His bulky winter coat and scarf made him look even larger. He stood quiet and stoic. He held a tight nervous grip on his wool cap with both hands. I stood to greet him. The man just stared down at my dad lying in bed, almost as if he were in some kind of trance.

"Hello?" I whispered.

That got the attention of my mom and brother, who, until this moment, didn't realize we had a guest. After a moment, the man snapped out of his trance. His eyes darted toward me.

"Oh, I'm sorry," he said, glancing back at my dad. "It's just a lot to take in."

"You're not kidding," my brother murmured.

For that, my mom gave him a swift tap on the shoulder. She got out of her seat to greet this massive stranger.

"Hi, I'm Diane, Richard's wife. And you are?"

He extended his hand. "Tyrese. Tyrese Dover. But you can just call me Dover."

"Nice to meet you, Dover. Do you work with my husband?"

"Nice to meet you too, ma'am. Yeah, I'm a driver," he replied. He seemed a bit shaken up.

"Well, please, come in," she said as if inviting him into her home.

He walked in slowly. For Dover, it wasn't more than a couple of steps from the doorway to my dad's bedside. He towered over the bed, still holding his wool cap in his hands.

"I can't believe this happened," Dover said. "Richie's a good guy."

"Do you know him well?" my mom asked.

"Oh, yeah," he replied. "He has always been good to me. He helped me through a rough time in my life."

"How so?" my mom asked.

"I was struggling, in debt up to my knees. I had to sell my car, my father's gold watch, everything. I started to take the bus to work." He smirked briefly. "Isn't that ironic? A bus driver taking the bus to work. The thing about buses is that they can be late and, on more than one occasion, caused me to clock in late. Richie kept asking me why I was late, but I made up excuse after excuse. I didn't want to get busted. Then I hit rock bottom."

We all listened intently as this man poured his soul out to us.

"I got a notice in the mail one day," Dover continued. "The bank was going to take my house. It wasn't much, but it was mine, you know? I put everything I had into that house. It was a part of me. That's when I gave up. I remember opening a bottle of Jack and not stopping until I saw the bottom. Then another bottle and another. I didn't show up to work for days. I guess, after a couple days, Richie came looking for me. He looked up my address from my contact info, which he really wasn't supposed to do, and came to my house looking for me. He was the last person I expected to see when I opened my front door."

He took a slight pause. He started to get emotional. His eyes began to water.

"He was the only one who bothered to check on me. He knocked some sense into me and helped me clean up my act. He convinced me to come back to work. He gave me bus fare, helped me sort out some of my expenses, helped me refinance my house, open a 401(k), everything. I was able to save my house because of him. Soon I was able to buy a car. It's nothing special, but it keeps me from taking the bus every day."

My mom, overwhelmed with pride in her husband, choked back tears. She put her hand on his arm and said, "Sounds like he really helped you out."

He turned and looked down toward her. A single tear ran down his cheek. "He saved me."

Both Dover and my mom hugged. I became emotional once again. My dad never failed to amaze me. It was truly inspirational how he looked after his coworkers in their times of need. He didn't have to. Their burdens weren't his to bear. Yet time and again, he stepped up to the plate, ready to lend a helping hand. Throughout my teenage years, we would argue. I may have had a hard time understanding his lessons or thought they were unfair, but in that moment looking back, I knew my life could not have been in greater hands. I vowed to myself, no matter the outcome, good or bad, that I would never stop striving to live up to my father—to honor him every day of my life.

We quietly conversed for a while. We swapped stories, shared a couple of laughs, and shed a few tears. Dover asked about all of us and how we were doing. He said he heard a lot about us from my dad. I honestly wish I could say the same about him, but I was glad he crossed paths with us. He brought an entirely new side of my dad into light. It really was getting late, and we were all tired. We decided to head home. Before leaving, my mom had one more question for Dover.

"Dover, by the way, do you know a guy by the name of Jerry Russo?"

"Jerry? Oh, sure! People down at the depot can't stop talking about the job he did on Richie when he went down."

"We heard as well. I don't think we would be here right now if it wasn't for him. I would like to meet him to thank him in person, but I haven't seen him."

My mom made a good point. I have heard all about this man's heroics and wanted to thank him as well, but there was no sign of him.

"Oh, he must have come, probably at night after his shift ends. He's been working doubles a lot lately so he can buy his motorcycle a new engine or something."

"Oh, okay. That makes sense."

With that out of the way, it was time to say good night. Dover walked us out like a bodyguard, and we parted ways. It was dark as ever. The icy wind howled in our faces. We braved the cold to reach our car parked down the street. I jumped inside to start the engine and crank up the heat. The leather seats were like ice. The windshield frosted over. My brother and my mom huddled inside as I scraped the ice off the windshield. Eventually we made our way home. I don't know if it was the cold, the late hour, or the weight of the past two weeks; but when we got home, we all passed out. It was the first decent sleep I could remember.

The next day, we arrived in the late morning. We left a little later in hopes of catching the end of the morning traffic. As usual, we greeted the nurses and staff as we walked by. They would always give us a friendly hello and smile in return. To our surprise, we entered my dad's room to a young couple already sitting down. It always seemed that we were the first to arrive. We were not used to walking in on people, so it made us jump a little. They quickly stood up out of their chairs. Both were tall and dark. They looked to be in their late twenties with athletic builds.

"Hello, I'm sorry if we startled you guys," the man said.

"No, no," I said, "you're good."

"I'm Sean, and this is my fiancé, Denise. We work with Richie."

Ah, that explained it. I wasn't sure where they knew him from, judging by their civilian attire.

"Hi, I'm Brian, his oldest son," I said as I turned to introduce the family. "This is my mom, Diane, and my younger brother, Kevin."

Not a second after I finished that sentence, Denise jumped forward to wrap her arms around my mom.

"Diane, I am so sorry. Are you doing okay?"

My mom was not expecting that hug.

"Oh…uh, yes, I guess we're hanging in there," she said, still in Denise's grasp.

Once she broke free, we were able to take off our coats and make ourselves at home.

"I love what you've done with the place," Sean said with a smile, trying to break the ice a bit.

That was good for a quick chuckle. They went on to explain that they met at Triboro. He was a bus driver, and she was an administrative assistant. They hit it off instantly and got engaged just months after dating. Before they tied the knot, they wanted to buy a house. They were looking at Long Island, around where we lived. They didn't know much about buying a house or where to buy for that matter. My dad, always having to put his two cents in, pushed for our area, citing reasonable taxes and excellent schools. Both were true. He answered any questions they had about mortgages, financing, and anything else pertaining to being a homeowner. I wasn't surprised at this point. I did, however, get a little jealous. I was happy my dad was helping this young couple out, but this was the kind of thing I was hoping my dad would help Nicole and I with in the near future. It didn't seem fair that they received all that fatherly advice and I may very well have been cheated out of it.

They couldn't stay long. They both had to get ready for work. The two of them needed to clock as many hours as they could if they hoped to buy a house before they say "I do."

One group of people we never saw visit was family. They all lived out of state. My dad's closest relative was his older brother. He, however, lived in Florida and had a healthy fear of flying. He called periodically to get updates but would only fly up if the worst should happen.

It was a peaceful afternoon, not a cloud in the sky. The sun shined through the hospital room window, filling the room with light. It was quiet. My family and I used this time to try and find some inner peace, but it was short-lived. Out of nowhere, Aunt Kathy, my dad's younger sister, came bursting in, startling us all. She was always one to make an entrance. Here was no different. Like all the women on my dad's side of the family, she was short and stocky. Yet her steps were so quiet she got the jump on us.

"Kathy?" my mom questioned. "I wasn't expecting to see you."

Aunt Kathy, the admitted oddball of the family, was a born-again Christian. A few years ago, with her newfound faith, she suddenly moved to the heart of Pennsylvania, old Quaker territory. We didn't see much of her after that. She focused most of her time on working with the church.

"I left my current mission early to come see him for myself. Plus I wanted to see my two favorite nephews," she said as she gave me and my brother big hugs. She held us tight. I was thrown off by her strength.

"Nice to see you too, Aunt Kathy," I said as she squeezed me.

She then released me from her grip and said, "Sweetie, just call me Kathy. Hearing the word *aunt* makes me feel old. Ha-ha-ha."

My mom got slightly irritated with my aunt. After all this time, why did she decide now to come see her brother and his family?

"Kathy, I'm surprised you didn't come sooner," my mom said.

"Oh, well, I got here as soon as I could. It's not easy leaving El Salvador in a hurry."

"El Salvador?" we all replied at once.

"What were you doing in El Salvador?" Kevin asked.

"I was on a mission like I mentioned," Aunt Kathy said with a smile.

Aunt Kathy really did some great work for the world. She was always traveling the country—in this case, Central America—with her church building homes and helping the poor and the less fortunate. She sat down and told us all about her most recent trip to El Salvador to help children in need. Many children were forced to work down in the impoverished country. Some could barely afford clean clothes or food. Some children were forced to steal. Drug cartels would take advantage of these poor young children by offering them an escape from poverty. The only problem was they were then forced to work for the cartels. Boys as young as ten years old were taken from their homes and given machine guns, forced to do the cartel's bidding.

My aunt flew down with a busload of missionaries to provide a safe haven for children to acquire clean clothes, eat a hot meal, and seek medical attention. Between the cartels and the military police who were paid to look the other way, it was a very dangerous place. One evening, they set up a stand on the side of a dirt road supplied with fresh water for the locals. One thing Aunt Kathy was known for down there was handing out candy to the small children. Most children living down there had never even seen a piece of candy.

A group of five or six young children surrounded her with outstretched hands, begging for candy. They couldn't have been more than six years old. As they ran off, one little girl was stopped by a boy, no older than twelve years of age, holding a machine gun. He knocked her to the ground and tried to take her candy from her.

"Hey!" Aunt Kathy yelled. She drew the boy's attention away long enough for the little girl to scramble to her feet and run off. "If you want some candy, come get some."

She didn't speak their language, so she tried her best to use gestures to convey what she was saying. The boy then pointed the barrel of the gun toward her, but my aunt wasn't fazed. The boy reached out his hand, demanding candy.

"Oh, no. Drop the gun! No gun or no candy!"

The boy huffed and turned his back to her.

"Fine. More for me," she said.

She turned away, unwrapped a piece of candy, and plopped it in her mouth. The boy looked back at her over his shoulder. His cartel training was at odds with his inner longing to just be a kid. My aunt looked out the corner of her eye and slowly extended her hand in which she held a single piece of butterscotch in a shiny gold wrapper. It took a few seconds, but he gave in. He broke a smile, dropped the gun, ran over to her, and grabbed the butterscotch out of her hand.

"My God, Kathy! Weren't you afraid?" asked my mom.

"A little," she admitted. "But I knew the Lord was protecting me."

If you ask me, she was a little insane. She was lucky she didn't get shot. That's what I never understood about religious types. Was the Lord truly protecting her? What if that boy decided to pull the trigger? If you asked those poor children, I'm not so sure they would say the Lord was protecting them. The whole debate of "God's plan" was enough to make me steer clear of religion. Sure, I called myself a Catholic but only because my family raised me that way.

At the conclusion of her little story, my aunt focused her attention on her brother.

"You mind?" she asked my mom.

My mom shook her head and gestured for her to step forward. She slowly walked over to his bedside. She took my dad's hand in hers, closed her eyes, and began to pray. I couldn't help but to roll my eyes. My mom caught me from across the room and stared daggers at me, signaling me to cut it out. After a moment, we heard a quiet amen.

"You're always in my prayers, big brother," she said, opening her eyes. She then looked around the room. "How are you guys hanging in?"

"The best we can, I guess," I replied.

"Any good news?" Aunt Kathy asked.

"Let me see. We haven't heard a shred of good news in about…a week," my mom said, crossing her arms.

"Well, don't worry. God is watching over him."

"Oh, is he?" I said with a bit of an attitude. "Is this what God watching over someone looks like?"

"Brian!" shouted my mom.

My aunt raised her hand. "It's okay, Diane." She turned her attention toward me. "We just need faith, Brian."

That was it. I was done. I wasn't about to get sucked into this right now. With a huff, I dropped back in my chair and tried to disassociate myself from this conversation.

"You'll see, which is why I brought in the big guns."

I just had to hear this one.

"I enlisted the help of the Prayer Warriors."

"Prayer…Warriors?" my brother asked, making sure he heard right.

"Yes. Prayer Warriors."

Those words didn't sound right together. They were not meant to follow each other in the same sentence. Upon hearing that phrase, all I could picture was a squadron of nuns sporting green berets and camouflage face paint. Aunt Kathy went on to describe Prayer Warriors as a large network of Christians, herself included, stretching across the country and around even the globe, thousands upon thousands of people of all walks of life joined in unified prayer. Their reach was wide, and it was powerful. Putting other people's needs before their own, these warriors pray in unison for any individual or group in dire need of a miracle. With the advancement of the Internet, they became able to reach others and spread word of the most desperate cases needing prayer in record time.

"I told my warrior brothers and sisters about Richie and his condition. Thousands are praying for him to recover. You'll feel their power soon."

This was a lot to process. I had no idea a network such as this existed. Now that I knew what it was and what they do, I almost felt…uplifted. Knowing thousands of complete strangers were praying for our family felt nice. It felt good to know that people out there cared so much.

"Wow, that's…amazing," said my mom, trying to process it all. "Just curious, how long ago did you inform the others about Richard?"

"Um, a few days ago," my aunt replied. "Even with the Internet, it's going to take some time for the word to spread to everyone. Just give it time."

"Gotcha. Thank you so much for your help. We all appreciate it."

"No need to thank me. You're family."

"Where are you staying while you're in town? Do you want to stay with us? It would be nice having you."

"Thank you, but I've made arrangements with a friend back in Richmond Hill."

"I bet it would be nice to return to the old neighborhood."

Aunt Kathy sighed. "Yeah, it's been a while."

"Well, if you ever need anything, you know where to find us."

"Thank you."

We spent the rest of the afternoon catching up. Aunt Kathy wanted to hear all about what we were up to these past few years. I told her all about college, as did Kevin. I told her about my job at the auto shop. Of course, she had a ton of questions about Nicole and me. She told us about where she was living now—in the rolling Pennsylvania countryside, surrounded by mountaintops. She lived in a tight-knit community in a small house, no fences between neighbors. Everyone was so kind and friendly, a far cry from New Yorkers. We talked for hours. Day rolled into evening. Outside the window, the sky was painted with shades of orange, yellow, and pink. Sunset seemed to come earlier and earlier each day.

"I should get going," said Aunt Kathy. "I want to catch the bus before it gets too dark."

"Will we see you again?" I said.

"Of course," she replied. "I have to make sure I'm here when he wakes up so I can yell at him for scaring us all half to death!"

"Not before I do!" my mom swiftly replied.

Aunt Kathy gave us all hugs and kisses and said her goodbyes. My mom walked over to the window and stared at the vibrant sky. She put her hands on her hips, inhaled deeply, and exhaled slowly. After about a minute, she turned.

"I guess it's time we head out too. What do you guys think?"

"Sure," I said as my brother and I reached for our coats.

We packed up our belongings and said goodbye to Dad. My mom gave him a kiss on the forehead as she did every night. We headed for the door, but before we could step into the hallway, we were stopped in our tracks.

"James!" my mom proclaimed.

James and another gentleman stood right in front of us. They turned the corner to enter my dad's room at the exact moment we were trying to leave, which startled my mom.

"Oh! Sorry, guys. Didn't mean to scare you," said James.

"That's okay. We were just about to go home. We weren't expecting you," said my mom.

"Well, then it's good I caught you."

"Why? What's up?"

"We need to talk. Perhaps you guys should sit down."

"Oh," my mom said, "okay then."

We all turned around and took our seats. James entered the room followed by his friend.

"This is Jose Rojas. He's one of our mechanics down at the depot," said James, introducing the man beside him. "Jose, why don't you tell them what you told me?"

Jose stepped forward, a little nervous and unsure. He fidgeted and rubbed his hands together. They were stained with grease and covered in scratches going up his forearms. He spoke slowly due to his heavy accent.

"Okay. Hi. Um, the day after Richie heart attack, I saw the manager go to the empty cabinet. They put in a new de-defibrillator and take pictures. Then they take it away."

"Wait a minute. James, what is he trying to say?" my mom asked.

"Jose and a few other guys witnessed a manager or an executive from upstairs take the defibrillator from the office, put it in the cabinet where ours was supposed to be, take a picture to prove it was there, and then bring it back upstairs."

"Holy crap," my brother responded.

"James, are you saying they knew about the missing defibrillator?" my mom asked.

"We think so. They took the picture to cover it up so they can have proof it was there the entire time."

My mom sprung up from her seat. "My husband needed that defibrillator!" she said angrily after hearing this news. "Who knows how much time could have been saved if they didn't have to go get the one upstairs."

I stood up. "They can't get away with this! We should press charges, or sue, or…something!" I got so angry I could barely speak.

"I agree," James responded. "Jose here and a few of the other guys are willing to give testimonials, if you decide to go down that route."

"It's not right," Jose chimed in. "Rich didn't deserve this. He's a good guy."

"Thank you, Jose," said my mom. "Do you really think we have a case?"

"We would like to get a hold of the security tapes showing them doing it, but yes, I think so," James replied. "I think you have a serious case for reckless endangerment. I just thought you guys should know."

"We need to sue their asses!" said Kevin.

"One thing at a time. Let's hope your dad wakes up. Then you can worry about seeing a lawyer," said James.

"We will," my mom said, turning her attention toward my brother and I. "Let's focus on your father for now and worry about this later."

We both agreed. We eased back on the idea of going to court, at least for now. Soon, however, we intended on going after them like a fire scorching the earth! The heartbreak my family endured would not go unavenged!

CHAPTER 10

I WAS RESTLESS THAT NIGHT when we got home. Most nights leading up to now, I felt fatigued, perhaps numb, and desired seclusion. This night didn't feel like most nights. I couldn't wrap my head around it, but it felt bigger, like there was more at stake. After everyone went to bed, I stayed up in my room, pacing back and forth. I was so anxious. I didn't know what to do with myself. I felt conflicting emotions: anger, sadness, and confusion. There was so much to process from the day we just had.

I felt an internal conflict brewing deep within me, our interaction with Aunt Kathy through my whole belief system on its head. I didn't know what to believe or where to turn. In the heart of December, I began to sweat. I sat on the edge of my bed. I buried my face into my hands while bouncing my knee up and down wildly. I could picture some manager in a white-collared shirt placing a faux defibrillator in my dad's first aid cabinet. Aunt Kathy's voice rang in my ear. The heat of the moment overwhelmingly brought me to my knees. I knelt down on the floor at the edge of my bed. I closed my eyes and proceeded to do something I never thought I would do.

I prayed.

I prayed to God and begged him to give me my dad back, to make my family whole again. There was so much I didn't know, so much he had left to teach me. I needed him. I missed him so much. I pleaded. I said I would do anything to have him back. I asked God to watch over him and my family but especially my mom. She was trying to be strong, but I didn't know how much more she could take.

Capped off with an amen, I finished talking to God. I reopened my eyes. Tears stained my face. My eyes were red, and yet I felt at ease. All the stress and anxiety seemed to have melted away. I could breathe easy once again. I stood up and took a breath. What a difference! I was ready to scream just a few minutes ago, and now it felt like a weight had been lifted off my shoulders. Could this be...could I be witnessing...the power of prayer? It must be. It felt good. I was finally able to rest easy. I got into bed and knocked out as soon as my head hit the pillow.

The next morning, I woke feeling refreshed, better than I felt in a long time. I felt an unfamiliar sense of optimism, one of which I hadn't felt in quite a while. I walked into the kitchen where I spotted my brother spoon deep in a large bowl of cereal.

"Good morning," I said with a smile.

"Why are you so chipper?" he asked with his mouth full.

"I don't know. Today just feels different."

"Okay," he said, rolling his eyes before digging back into his breakfast.

As soon as we all had breakfast and got dressed, we hit the road again. My car racked on some serious mileage through all this and was burning a lot of gas sitting in rush-hour traffic every morning. It was a small price to pay in order to see my dad every day. It was a beautiful day, which made the traffic much more bearable. It took us over an hour to get there, but it didn't feel as long, at least not to me.

It was quiet when we got there. The ICU had become noticeably quieter compared to the first days we arrived. I noticed far less cries of agony from loved ones. Or perhaps now I had become numb to it. Either way, as we made our way down the hall, I saw a lot more empty beds. In here, I learned that could be a good thing or a bad thing.

We sat for hours as per usual. Nothing was really going on. We didn't have a single visitor. To help pass the time, my mom took to reading books. She was on her third one currently. My brother brought magazines and even broke out the old Game Boy. I mostly stuck to social media. I liked to draw, so I brought along a sketch pad some days. Aunt Kathy called a couple of times but never came. I guess she had other plans. She was the kind of woman you just couldn't put your finger on—here one day and gone the next, more like a born-again drifter rather than a born-again Christian.

Nothing had changed since the day before. In fact, not much had changed in the past week. We decided to cut our stay short and head home early. My mom had some bills to pay. My dad always took care of the bills in our house, but my mom got pretty adept to doing it in his absence. Once again, we walked down the hall to the elevator, waving goodbye to every nurse and doctor along the way. We made it to the elevator, got inside, and made our way down to the street.

Back in the ICU, everything was calm. All the nurses' rounds were complete for the day, so they huddled in the nurses' station. From there, they could monitor all of the patient's vitals displayed on various screens placed all around them. They were differentiated by room number displayed on the top of each screen. The nurses all had their heads down filing paperwork and going over patient notes. Suddenly an alarm sounded! It startled the nurses. Their eyes scrambled to find the screen where it was coming from. They spun their heads and stared directly at the screen linked to 12A. My dad's vitals were jumping violently all over the place! The screen flashed red everywhere. Then suddenly, everything went blank. His blood pressure and oxygen levels dropped to zero. His heartbeat, flatlined.

The nurses went into red alert. They jumped from their seats and flew down the hall. Nancy, the veteran, jumped behind a crash cart and pushed with everything she had. The first nurses ran into his room but froze in disbelief. Nancy dug her heels into the floor to keep the crash cart from running them over.

The soles of her shoes screeched along the linoleum floor as the cart came to a stop.

"What the hell are you doing?" Nancy cried.

Her fellow nurses didn't respond. They just stood there frozen in shock. Nancy pushed past them to see what was going on. Even with all she had seen in her long career, she, too, couldn't believe what she was looking at.

We had just made it to the car and were driving down the street when my mom's cell phone began to ring. She rummaged through her purse for it.

"Ah, come on," she said, sifting through her bag. She found it at the last second. "Hello?"

There was a short period of silence. Her eyes widened, and her jaw dropped as she listened to the person at the other end of that call.

"Turn around," she whispered.

"What?" I questioned.

"Turn around! Right now! Turn around!"

Without hesitation, I immediately jerked the wheel. The tires lost their grip. Smoke poured from the bottom of the car as I flung it 180 degrees. My brother, in the back not wearing his seatbelt, was flung against the glass. I slammed the gas pedal and flew down the residential street back toward the hospital. When I heard the tone of my mother's voice, I didn't question her demands. I just reacted.

A nurse had called to break the news. My dad was awake! His eyes sprung open. His once-lifeless body came alive. He grabbed the breathing tube, which was shoved down his throat, and triumphantly pulled it out himself. When the nurses ran in, they locked eyes with my dad. Holding the breathing tube in his hand, he extended his arm toward the nurses as if to say "Here you go!"

We ran inside, up to the seventh floor, and down the hall. We gathered just outside the hospital room. We couldn't believe what we were looking at. It was true. We were admittedly skeptical at first. We had letdowns before, but there he was. Nurses were hovering over him, checking everything they could. They were as shocked as we were. I never thought I would be so happy to see his eyes. But was it him? Was he all there? Would he recognize us? My mom entered with a few cautious steps. Out of the corner of his eye, he saw her and slowly turned his head toward us.

"Richard?" she gently prodded.

He didn't answer right away. The nurses all froze in place. An eerie silence filled the air. His face was blank. He just stared at her for a moment. And then, he smiled.

"Hey, hun."

Chapter 11

The next morning, we all gathered around his bed—I, my brother, my mom, and Aunt Kathy. Even James came to share in this joyous occasion. Laughter and smiles filled the room. The only tears flowing now were tears of joy. My mom stood right by my dad's side and wouldn't let go of his hand. Dr. Peterson ran a multitude of tests; but aside from a raspy voice from the tube down his throat, he was perfectly fine—no brain damage and no paralysis, nothing. There was barely even any muscle loss from being in bed for so long. The doctor was utterly shocked. He couldn't wrap his head around it. It was truly a miracle.

Dr. Peterson got my dad up to speed. He explained that his condition, HOCM, caused his heart to stop and explained that it can be hereditary. He performed a host of physical and cognitive tests. He tested both eyes and both ears and asked him to touch his fingers to his nose and for him to wiggle his toes.

"Well, Mr. Pellegrino," Dr. Peterson said, "I never thought I would say this, but you have a clean bill of health. What I strongly recommend is we implant a defibrillator-pacemaker combo in your chest to prevent this from ever happening again."

"Whatever you say, Doc," my dad replied.

"Will that keep him here much longer?" my mom asked.

She was just about done with this hospital and wanted her husband home as soon as possible.

"It is a reasonably simple procedure. I would like to keep him here for a couple more days after it's completed so we can keep an eye on him. Then I think I'll have no problem sending him home."

"Eh, what's a couple of days?" my dad said, to which my mom gave him a dirty look.

"Yeah, try a couple of weeks," my mom scoffed.

Everyone laughed.

Dr. Peterson decided to step out to give us some privacy. "I'll be back in a few hours to check on you."

"Thank you, Doctor," my mom said.

He gave a nod of his head and left.

"I can't believe it. Was it really a couple of weeks?" my dad asked.

"The longest two weeks of our lives," I said.

"Do you really have no idea how you got here?" James questioned in disbelief.

"No, not at all. The last thing I remember is being at work. The next thing I know, I woke up here with that damn tube down my throat."

He rubbed his throat after saying that. It was still sore from the breathing tube. No wonder why he yanked it out the first chance he had.

"You were very near death, Richie," said Aunt Kathy.

"Huh. I guess I would have died and never even known it."

That all gave us a quick laugh.

"That's one way to put it," my mom said, smiling through a last bit of tears.

"It's safe to say you had someone watching over you," said my aunt.

My dad took a moment to let that sink in.

"I know at least one person who was looking out for you. Jerry," Kevin said.

"Jerry? Jerry Russo? The EMT?"

"Yes," my mom replied. "He brought you back after you collapsed at your desk. If not for him"—she paused and looked up at her boys—"we might not be here right now."

"I'll have to be sure to thank him."

"Me too. I still haven't had the chance," said Mom.

"I don't know where he's been, but I haven't seen him in a couple of days. The next time I see him, I'll be sure to pass on the good news," said James.

Time went by, and conversations flowed. As my mom and dad were catching up and James was chewing my brother's ear off about who knows what, Aunt Kathy pulled me aside.

"Isn't this a miracle?" she said, smiling ear to ear.

"Yes, I would say so," I replied.

"I could sense your skepticism when I spoke of faith the other day."

My face turned red with embarrassment. I was a fool to doubt her faith. It also was extremely rude to do it so openly. I hoped she wouldn't hold it against me.

"Yeah, I'm sorry. I was wrong."

"I know you're sorry. It's okay. I don't know how, but I have a feeling that now you see what the power of faith can do."

I took a moment to let that sink in. She was right. Something deep within me had changed, and I think for the better. I looked over to my dad sitting up in bed, chatting and smiling with my mom. "Yeah, I think you're right."

That night, they began to prep him for surgery. If everything went well, he was going to stay one more full day and night, then he could finally come home. My mom insisted we'd stay, but my dad said otherwise. He could see we were all exhausted and sent us home to sleep in our own beds.

"I'm not going anywhere," he said to us.

It took some convincing, but we agreed to go home to recuperate. For the first time when we gave him hugs goodbye, he was able to hug us back. What a great feeling that was, a feeling that I took for granted in the past but certainly no longer.

We eagerly waited by the phone that night for the call to inform us that he was out of surgery. The phone rang just before 9:00 p.m. The surgery was a success, and he was resting comfortably. We all breathed a sigh of relief. We were one step closer to ending this whole thing. For the first time in a long while, we could all sleep easy. I, on the other hand, had one thing I had to do before I could get some shut-eye. In the privacy of my bedroom, I knelt down at the edge of my bed once again. With my mind at ease, I prayed once again. I thanked God for answering my prayers. I thanked him for making my family whole. I would never forget the lessons I learned.

Two days later, we made our last trip out to Queens. If I never saw that hospital again, I would be perfectly fine with that. In the true Christmas spirit, we came bearing gifts for all of the nurses and hospital staff. They were so good to us and did an amazing job. We were amazed by the level of care and professionalism they displayed. We just wanted to give back. It was the least we could do. We stepped off the elevator wrestling with an abundance of gift baskets filled with fruits, chocolates, and other holiday treats. Everyone's faces lit up when we handed them their gift basket. They don't do it for the praise, but like anyone else, it feels good to be appreciated.

My dad was sitting at the edge of the bed. He was as ready to get back home as we were. He showed us the incision they made in his chest. It was surprisingly small, about two inches long. What skeeved me out was that, if he moved a certain way, you could see the outline of the defibrillator under his skin, about-a-one-inch rectangle with rounded points.

After a few hours, they finally handed him his discharge papers, which he was happy to sign. A nurse came with a wheelchair to help him to the front door.

He did lose some strength in his legs after lying horizontal for so long. He leaned off the bed and, like a baby deer learning to walk his legs, wobbled; but he stood up. It felt good to see him on his feet. I almost forgot how tall he was. He towered over me. I went ahead to pull the car around to the front of the hospital. I pulled up the second they were pushing my dad out the front door. He insisted on taking the front seat. My mom and brother were happy to grant him his wish and hopped in the back. I made sure to drive extra careful on the way home. If my dad witnessed my driving on that first morning, he would have killed me.

Finally we arrived home. My dad leaned against me and my brother as we made our way down the front walk and up the steps of the front porch. As we walked through the door, the house felt different. It didn't feel as dark and dreary but bright and full of life. It was just missing one thing.

"Eddie!" I exclaimed.

To my surprise, we were greeted by our ninety-pound Labrador mere seconds after stepping through the front door. I knelt down and grabbed him before he could jump on my dad. He was so full of excitement I could barely contain him. His tail spun like a helicopter, and it didn't seem like he could keep his feet on the ground.

"What are you doing here?"

"I called Carol when we were about to leave the hospital," my mom said, holding my dad's arm in hers. "I thought it would be nice to have him home waiting for us, so I told her where to find the spare key, and she dropped him off. The family is finally whole again."

"Hey, you didn't decorate the tree," my dad said when he caught a glimpse of the living room.

"Oh, yeah, we didn't," said Kevin.

"Why not?"

"We wanted to wait until you made it home," I said.

"Well, let's get started," said my dad eagerly.

"We can decorate it," my mom said to my dad. "You can sit and watch. You need to rest."

"Whatever you say, dear."

We helped my dad over to the couch. Eddie jumped up next to him and wedged himself under his arm. His tail beat the cushion like a drum. Kevin and I broke out the storage bins filled with lights and ornaments. First we strung the lights and then came the ornaments. My dad looked on with glee. He remained silent for the most part. Occasionally he would bark an order for us to move something to, in his mind, a better location. That's the kind of man he was. Usually I would get frustrated, but now? I didn't mind one bit. Normally it was my dad's job to put the star on top of the tree as he was the tallest. The honor this year fell to my brother. He proudly placed the beautiful white-and-gold star atop our tree. Down below, I grabbed the end of the wire and plugged it into the outlet. The five of us gathered on the couch and just stared at our beautiful tree with its shimmering star sitting on top.

There were a lot of memories made during this time that will stay with me forever. Most of them I'll admit are negative, some extremely so, although, that moment in front of the tree—that first moment of all of us together huddling around my dad on the couch in the living room, sitting in the glow of our freshly decorated tree—that is a memory I will cherish for the rest of my life. There are many peaks and valleys in life, highs and lows, and good times and bad. Through all of it, focus only on the good. Cherish all the precious moments you can in life because you never know what might be waiting for you—at the edge of a heartbeat.

Epilogue

My family, for obvious reasons, didn't have time to do much Christmas shopping; so the number of gifts under the tree on Christmas morning was fairly minimal. Nevertheless, that didn't stop it from being the best Christmas I could remember. I got everything I needed. Dad received the greatest Christmas gift of all—the gift of life. He made a speedy recovery. That morning, he woke up early to make pancakes for everyone. Eddie eagerly sat by his feet hoping to catch a scrap or two on its way to the floor.

As for his job, my dad officially retired there in that hospital bed after waking up. It was time to stay home and keep that heart as stress-free as possible. There still was the matter of legal action against his company. My parents sought out a lawyer to see if they had a case. The lawyer they sat down with explained their case unfortunately would have been stronger if the company's negligence resulted in permanent injury or death. Lucky for us, that wasn't the case. Also, the surveillance tapes were never obtained. Without video evidence, the lawyer advised that, yes, they could pursue charges, but the company's extensive legal team would drag it along in the courts for years, and it would cost my parents a small fortune.

After a long discussion, my parents agreed not to pursue charges. This meant less of a headache for our family, which had already been through so much. As a gesture of good faith, the company paid to have my dad's Cadillac, which had been sitting in the parking lot this entire time, towed home from Queens so we didn't have to go pick it up.

AFTER CHRISTMAS, I WAS EAGER to return to work. I called the shop to tell them the good news that I would be coming back, but no one answered. I didn't think much of it. They were probably too busy to pick up the phone. It was a few minutes away, so I decided to take a drive and talk to them in person.

I pulled up to the shop. Normally, by this time in the afternoon, it would be bustling; but the parking lot was empty. The inside was dark, and the door was locked. This didn't make sense. Old Paul would never close the shop on a weekday afternoon. They needed the business.

I walked around to the back door to see if the garage was open. As I turned the corner, I saw that the garage door was indeed closed as well. Not only that, but my toolbox sat on the ground in front of it. Something clearly wasn't right. I knelt beside it and noticed a piece of paper tucked under the handle. It was a note from Laura Morris. It read:

Dear Brian,

> We wish you and your family all the luck in the world. You did the right thing choosing your family over this old place.

Either one of us would have done the same. By now, you have noticed that the shop is closed. Unfortunately, with your absence, the workload was too much for Paul. He tried his hardest to keep the shop going, but his old body kept quitting on him. We decided it would be best to sell and enjoy our retirement. Don't you worry about us, and please know this wasn't your fault. This was a long time coming. If you ever need a reference, you make sure to put down our number. And remember, family first.

Always,

Laura and Paul

I couldn't believe it. It was hard for me not to think that I was the reason they were forced to sell. I learned a lot working here and really hated to see it go. I was going to miss the Morrises as well. I remembered what the note said—not to blame myself and focus on family. So I put the note in my pocket, picked up my toolbox, and carried it to my car. I put it in the trunk and got in. Just as I was about to turn the key, I realized something.

"Oh, crap! I need to find a new job!"

WHAT BECAME OF JERRY RUSSO, the man who saved my dad's life in what seemed like a lifetime ago? We never got the chance to thank him. Jerry had just finished his motorcycle and headed out on the road to see a buddy of his upstate. Unfortunately, he never made it. It was below freezing that day, and the roads were icy. That wasn't enough to keep Jerry from doing what he loved, however. On his way up north, one of his tires caught a patch of black ice right after crossing the Tappan Zee Bridge. He lost control and collided with the center median at over sixty miles per hour. His body sustained heavy injuries. He was rushed to the hospital, where he would die of internal bleeding.

We were in shock when we heard the tragic news. This shouldn't have happened. The man saved a life to just lose his own. That didn't seem fair. We were never going to get the chance to tell Jerry, my dad especially, how grateful we were to him. The best my dad could do was thank his wife, Veronica, at the funeral. Her face lit up when my dad told his story. She smiled through the tears, proud of her husband. It's memories like those we need to hold on to because it is in those memories where our loved ones live on.

About the Author

BRIAN PELLEGRINO, BORN IN 1993, comes from a middle-class Long Island family. He currently lives in Farmingdale, New York, with his lovely wife, Nicole. Brian worked as an auto mechanic to put himself through college but never found it fulfilling. He always knew he was destined for something greater. Being his high school sweetheart, Nicole motivated Brian to follow his dreams. That was the push he needed in order to share his story with the world. Growing up with a stutter, Brian would find it difficult to communicate at times but found solace in conveying his thoughts through written word.

His many interests include a love of dogs, cars, trying new restaurants, and cruising around the world. Brian is a loyal and devoted friend. To him, his close friends are like family, and he enjoys traveling the country with them or just hanging out in the backyard discussing life over a beer.